BE SUCCESSFUL

Be Successful

WARREN W. WIERSBE

While this book is intended for the reader's personal enjoyment and profit, it is also designed for group study. Study questions are located at the end of the text.

Run So That You May Win
ivictor.com

Victor is an imprint of
Cook Communications Ministries, Colorado Springs, Colorado 80918
Cook Communications, Paris, Ontario
Kingsway Communications, Eastbourne, England

BE SUCCESSFUL
© 2001 by Warren W. Wiersbe

First Printing, 2001
Printed in the United States of America

1 2 3 4 5 6 7 8 9 10 Printing/Year 05 04 03 02 01

Editors: Barbara Williams; Craig Bubeck, Sr. Editor
Cover Design: iDesignEtc.

CONTENTS

PREFACE

What is success? Some say it's simply achieving your goals, but how do we know those goals were worth achieving? Are you a success if you reach contemptible goals by dishonorable means? Some spell success with dollar signs—$UCCE$$—but if money is the measure of success, then Jesus was a dismal failure. Adolph Hitler had a frightening definition of success: "the sole and earthly judge of right and wrong." In short, might makes right.

First Samuel is a book about success and failure, both in individuals and in a nation. The nation of Israel failed. Eli and his sons were failures. King Saul started out a success but soon became a failure. David was a success in his character, conduct, and service. He was a man after God's own heart.

Actually, success is a by-product. "Try not to become a man of success," wrote Albert Einstein, "but rather try to become a man of value." Values involve character, which is why Theodore Roosevelt said, "The chief factor in any man's success or failure must be his own character." Eli, the priest, and Saul, the king, both had reputations; but David had character. His character and skills were developed in private before they were demonstrated in public.

Until individuals, churches, and nations start emphasizing character and obedience, there can never be true success. Only through faith in Jesus Christ and obedience to His will can we have godly character and the kind of success that will survive the fires of God's judgment. What was true of King Uzziah can be also true of us: "As long as he sought the Lord, God gave him success" (2 Chron. 26:5, NIV).

Warren W. Wiersbe

A Suggested Outline of 1 Samuel

Key Theme: The establishment of a king in Israel
Key Verse: 1 Samuel 12:22

I. The failure of the priesthood—1–7

The birth of Samuel—1:1–2:11
The failure of Eli—2:12-36
The call of Samuel—3
The rescue of the ark—4–6
The new spiritual beginning—7

II. The failure of the first king—8–15

Israel requests a king—8
Saul is made king—9–10
Saul's first victories—11
The nation renews the covenant—12
Saul loses the throne—13–15

III. The training of the new king—16–31

David is anointed—16:1-13
David serves Saul—16:14-23
David kills Goliath—17
Saul becomes jealous of David—18–19
The love of David and Jonathan—20
David driven into exile—21–27, 29–30
Saul's defeat and death—28; 31

A Suggested Timeline

1105 B.C.   The birth of Samuel

1080 B.C.   The birth of Saul

1050 B.C.   Saul anointed king

1040 B.C.   Birth of David

1025 B.C.   David anointed king

1010 B.C.   Death of Saul

1010-1003 B.C. David reigns in Hebron

1003-970 B.C.   David reigns over all Israel

"The Lord of Hosts Is with Us"

One of the awesome titles of our great God is "Lord of Hosts" or "Lord of the armies." This title is used nearly 300 times in Scripture and is found for the first time in 1 Samuel 1:3. "Lord of hosts" describes God as the sovereign Lord of the host of the stars (Isa. 40:26), the angelic host (Ps. 103:20-21) and the armies of Israel (Ex. 12:41; Ps. 46:7, 11). In the *Authorized Version*, "hosts" is transliterated "Sabaoth" in Romans 9:29 and James 5:4. In his hymn "A Mighty Fortress Is Our God," Martin Luther rightly applied this title to Jesus Christ:

> Did we in our own strength confide,
> Our striving would be losing,
> Were not the right Man on our side,
> The Man of God's own choosing.
> Dost ask who that may be?
> Christ Jesus, it is He;
> Lord Sabaoth His name,
> From age to age the same,
> And He must win the battle.

The story of the people of Israel recorded in the Bible is a living demonstration of the fact that the Lord *does* win the battle, that He is sovereign in all things. People and events recorded in Scripture are part of what theologians call "salvation history," God's gracious plan to send the Savior into the world to die for sinners. The Book of Ruth ends with the name of David (Ruth 4:22), and 1 Samuel tells the story of David's successful preparation for reigning on the throne of Israel. It was from David's family that Jesus Christ, the "Son of David," was born. The Books of Samuel, Kings, and Chronicles record many sins and failures on the part of God's people, but they also remind us that God is on the throne, and when He isn't allowed to rule, He overrules. He is the Lord of Hosts and His purposes will be accomplished.

1. God directs history

"What are all histories but God manifesting Himself," said Oliver Cromwell over three centuries ago, but not everybody agrees with him. The British historian Edward Gibbon, who wrote *The Decline and Fall of the Roman Empire*, called history "little more than the register of crimes, follies, and misfortunes of mankind," and Lord Chesterfield, his contemporary, called history "a confused heap of facts." But Dr. A.T. Pierson, preacher and missionary statesman of the last century, said it best when he wrote, "History is His story." This is particularly true of the history recorded in the Bible, for there we have the inspired account of the hand of God at work in the affairs of mankind to bring the Savior into the world.

The Book of Judges is the book of "no king" and describes a nation in which anarchy was the norm. "In those days there was no king in Israel, but every man did that which was right in his own eyes" (Jud. 17:6; and see 18:1; 19:1; and 21:25). Israel wasn't a united people, as during the days of Joshua, but it was a loose confederation of tribes with God-appointed judges ruling in widely separated areas. There was no standing army nor were there permanent military leaders. Men from the different tribes volunteered to defend the land when they were summoned to battle.

But during those dark days of the Judges, a love story took place that's recorded in the Book of Ruth. Boaz married Ruth the Moabitess and from their union came Obed, the father of Jesse who became the father of David the king. *There was no king in Israel, but God was already at work preparing the way for His chosen servant* (Ps. 78:56-72). If Judges is the book of "no king," then 1 Samuel is the book of "man's king." The people of Israel asked for a king and God gave them Saul, from the tribe of Benjamin, who turned out to be a tragic failure. But the Lord had prepared David for the throne, and 2 Samuel is the book of "God's king."

You cannot read the records of the past without seeing the hand of "the Lord of Hosts" at work in the events of what we call history. The Lord is mentioned over sixty times in 1 Samuel 1–3, for He is the chief actor in this drama. Men and women are free to make their decisions, good or bad, but it is Jehovah, the Lord of history, who ultimately accomplishes His purposes in and through the nations (Acts 14:15-17; 17:24-26; Dan. 4:25, 32). Indeed, "history is His story," a truth that is a great encouragement to God's people who suffer for their faith. But this truth is also a warning to unbelievers who ignore or oppose the will of God, because the Lord of hosts will ultimately triumph.

Samuel was God's "bridge builder" at a critical time in Jewish history when the weak confederation of tribes desperately needed direction. He was the last of the judges (1 Sam. 7:15-17; Acts 13:20) and the first of a new line of prophets after Moses (3:24). He established a school of the prophets, and he anointed two kings—Saul who failed and David who succeeded. At a time when the ages were colliding and everything seemed to be shaking, Samuel gave spiritual leadership to the nation of Israel and helped to move them toward national unification and spiritual rededication.

In human history, it may appear to us that truth is "forever on the scaffold" and wrong is "forever on the throne," but that isn't heaven's point of view. As you study 1 Samuel, you will see clearly that God is always in control. While He is long-suffering and merciful and answers the prayers of His people, He is also holy and just and punishes sin. We live today in a time of radical worldwide change, and the church needs leaders like Samuel who will help God's people understand where they've been, who they are, and what they are called to do.

2. God answers prayer (1 Sam. 1:1-28)

During the period of the judges, the Israelites were in dire straits because they lacked godly leadership. The priesthood was defiled, there was no sustained prophetic message from the Lord (3:1), and the Law of Moses was being ignored throughout the land. As He often did in Israel's history, God began to solve the problem by sending a baby. Babies are God's announcement that He knows the need, cares about His people, and is at work on their behalf. The arrival of a baby ushers in new life and a new beginning; babies are signposts to the future, and their conception and birth is a miracle that only God can do (Gen. 30:1-2). To make the event seem even greater, God sometimes selects barren women to be the mothers, as when He sent Isaac to Sarah, Jacob and Esau to Rebekah, and Joseph to Rachel.

A divided home (1 Sam. 1:1-8). Elkanah was a Levite, a Kohathite from the family of Zuph (1 Chron. 6:22-28, 34-35). The Levites were scattered throughout the land and went to Shiloh to minister at the tabernacle whenever they were needed. Elkanah lived in Ramah on the border of Ephraim and Benjamin (see Josh. 18:25). Elkanah's famous son Samuel would be born in Ramah (1 Sam. 1:19-20), live there (7:17), and be buried there when he died (25:1).[1]

In many ways, Elkanah seems to be a good and godly man, except that he had two wives. Apparently Hannah was his first wife, and when she proved barren, he married Peninnah so he could have a family. We don't know why Elkanah didn't wait on the Lord and trust Him to work out His plan, but even Abraham married Hagar (Gen. 16) and Jacob ended up with four wives! While bigamy and divorce were not prohibited by Jewish law (Deut. 21:15-17; 24:1-4), God's original plan was that one man be married to one woman for one lifetime (Mark 10:1-9).

Each year Elkanah took his family to Shiloh to worship (Ex. 23:14-19), and together they ate a meal as a part of their worship (Deut. 12:1-7). This annual visit to the tabernacle should have been a joyful event for Hannah, but each year Peninnah used it as an opportunity to irritate her rival and make fun of her barrenness. When Elkanah distributed the meat from the sacrifice, he had to give many portions to Peninnah and her children, while Hannah received only one portion. Elkanah gave her a generous share, but his generosity certainly didn't compensate for her infertility. [2]

The name "Hannah" means "a woman of grace," and she did manifest grace in the way she dealt with her barrenness and Peninnah's attitude and cruel words. Elkanah was able to have children by Peninnah, so Hannah knew that the problem lay with her and not with her husband. It seemed unfair that a woman with Peninnah's ugly disposition should have many children while gracious Hannah was childless. She also knew that only the Lord could do for her what he did for Sarah and Rachel, but why had God shut up her womb? Certainly this experience helped to make her into a woman of character and faith and motivated her to give her best to the Lord. She expressed her anguish only to the Lord and she didn't create problems for the family by disputing with Peninnah. In everything she said and did, Hannah sought to glorify the Lord. Indeed, she was a remarkable woman who gave birth to a remarkable son.

A devout prayer (1 Sam. 1:9-18). During one of the festive meals at Shiloh, Hannah left the family and went to the tabernacle to pray. She had determined in her heart that the Lord wanted her to pray for a son so that she might give him back to the Lord to serve Him all his life. It's an awesome fact that, humanly speaking, the future of the nation rested with this godly woman's prayers; and yet, how much in history has depended on the prayers of suffering and sacrificing people, especially mothers.

The original tabernacle was a tent surrounded by a linen fence, but from the description in the text we learn that God's sanctuary now included some sort of wooden structure with posts

(1:9) and doors (3:2, 15) and in which people could sleep (vv. 1-3). This structure and the tabernacle together were called "the house of the Lord" (1:7), "the temple," "the tabernacle of the congregation," and God's "habitation" (2:32). It was here that aged Eli, the high priest, sat on his priestly throne to oversee the ministry, and it was there that Hannah went to pray. She wanted to ask the Lord for a son and to promise the Lord her son would serve Him all the days of his life.

What an example Hannah is in her praying! It was a prayer born out of sorrow and suffering, but in spite of her feelings, she laid bare her soul before the Lord. It was a prayer that involved submission, for she presented herself to the Lord as His handmaid, to do whatever He wanted her to do (see Luke 1:48). It was a prayer that also involved sacrifice, because she vowed to give her son back to the Lord, to be a Nazirite (Num. 6) and serve the Lord all his life. In praying like this, was Hannah "bargaining" with the Lord? I don't think so. Bearing a son would have removed her disgrace and perhaps ended her rival's persecution, but giving up the son was another matter. Perhaps it would have been easier for her to go on living in barrenness than to have a child for three years and have to give him up forever. I wonder if God had given Hannah an inner conviction that her son would play an important part in the future of the nation.

Hannah's faith and devotion were so strong that they rose above the misunderstanding and criticism of the nation's highest spiritual leader. When you give your best to the Lord, it's not unusual to be criticized by people who ought to encourage you. Moses was criticized by his brother and sister (Num. 12), David by his wife (2 Sam. 6:12-23), and Mary of Bethany by an apostle (John 12:1-8), yet all three were commended by the Lord. In the first four chapters of 1 Samuel, Eli comes across as a poor example of a believer, let alone a high priest. He was probably self-indulgent (4:18) and definitely tolerant of the sins of his two sons (2:22-36), and yet he was quick to judge and condemn the devotions of a godly woman. "In prayer it is better to have a heart without words, than words without a heart," said John Bunyan, and that's the way Hannah prayed.

Those who lead God's people need spiritual sensitivity so they can "rejoice with those who rejoice, and weep with those who weep" (Rom. 12:15 NKJV). Eli accused her of pouring out too much wine, when all she was doing was pouring out her soul to God in prayer (1 Sam. 1:15). Five times Hannah called herself a "handmaid," which signified her submission to the Lord and His servants. We don't read that Eli apologized to her for judging her so severely, but at least he gave her his blessing, and she returned to the feast with peace in her heart and joy on her countenance. The burden was lifted from her heart and she knew that God had answered her prayer.

A distinguished son (1 Sam. 1:19-28). When the priests offered the burnt offering early the next morning, Elkanah and his family were there to worship God, and Hannah's soul must have been rejoicing, for she had given herself as a living sacrifice to the Lord (Rom. 12:1-2). When the family arrived home, God answered her prayers and gave her conception, and when her child was born, it was a son whom she named Samuel. The Hebrew word *sa-al* means "asked," and *sama* means "heard," and *el* is one of the names for God, so Samuel means "heard of God" or "asked of God." All his life, Samuel was both an answer to prayer and a great man of prayer.[3]

Certainly Hannah told Elkanah about her vow, because she knew that Jewish law permitted a husband to annul a wife's vow if he disagreed with it (Num. 30). Elkanah agreed with her decision and allowed her to remain at home with her son when the rest of the family went on its annual trip to Shiloh. We can't help but admire Elkanah for what he said and did, for this was his firstborn son by his beloved Hannah and father and son would be separated for the rest of their lives. A firstborn son had to be redeemed by a sacrifice (Ex. 13:11-13), but Elkanah was giving his son as a living sacrifice to the Lord. As a Levite, a Nazirite, a prophet, and a judge, Samuel would faithfully serve the Lord and Israel and help to usher in a new era in Jewish history.

Mothers usually weaned children at the age of three, and surely during those precious years, Hannah taught her son and prepared him for serving the Lord. He did not have a personal knowledge of the Lord until later when God spoke to him (1 Sam. 3:7-10). Hannah was a woman of prayer (1:27) and taught her son to be a man of prayer. When she and Elkanah took their son to Shiloh to give him to the Lord, they brought along the necessary sacrifices so they could worship the Lord. The *Authorized Version* reads "three bullocks" while other translations read "a three-year-old bull" (NIV, NASB). However, the fact that the parents took a skin of wine and an ephah of meal, enough to accompany three sacrifices, suggests that three bullocks is the correct number, for three-tenths of an ephah of grain was needed for each bull sacrificed (Num. 28:12).

When Elkanah and Hannah presented their son to the Lord, Hannah reminded Eli that she was the woman who had prayed for a son three years before.[4] Did the old man remember the occasion and did he recall how unfairly he had dealt with this sorrowing woman? If he did, there's no record of it; but he received the boy to become a servant of the Lord at the tabernacle and be trained in the law of the Lord.

Considering the low level of spiritual life in Eli and the wicked ways of his sons, it took a great deal of faith for Elkanah and Hannah to leave their innocent son in their care. But the Lord was with Samuel and would preserve him from the pollution around him. Just as God protected Joseph in Egypt, so He would protect Samuel in Shiloh, and so He can protect our children and grandchildren in this present evil world. Judgment was coming to Eli and his family, but God would have Samuel prepared to guide the nation and move them into the next stage of their development.

The story thus far makes it clear that the life and future of a nation depends on the character of the home, and the character of the home depends on the spiritual life of the parents. An African proverb says, "The ruin of a nation begins in the homes of its people," and even Confucius taught, "The strength of a nation is derived from the integrity of its homes." Eli and his sons had "religious" homes that were godless, but Elkanah and Hannah had a godly home that honored the Lord, and they gave Him their best. The future hope of the people of Israel rested with that young lad in the tabernacle learning to serve the Lord. Never underestimate the power of the home or the power of a little child dedicated to God.

3. God receives praise and worship (1 Sam. 2:1-11)

After Hannah left her son with Eli, she could have gone off alone and had a good cry, but instead she burst into a song of praise to the Lord. The world doesn't understand the relationship between sacrifice and song, how God's people can sing their way into sacrifice and sacrifice their way into singing. "And when the burnt offering began, the song of the Lord began also" (2 Chron. 29:27, KJV). Before He went to the garden where He would be arrested, Jesus sang a hymn with His disciples (Matt. 26:30); and Paul and Silas sang hymns to the Lord after they had been humiliated and beaten (Acts 16:20-26). Frequently in the psalms you find David praising God in the midst of difficult circumstances. After being beaten by the religious leaders in Jerusalem, the apostles "departed from the presence of the council, rejoicing that they were counted worthy to suffer shame for His name" (Acts 5:41, NKJV).

Hannah's song near the beginning of 1 Samuel should be compared with David's song found near the end of 2 Samuel (22), as well as with Mary's song in Luke 1:46-55. All three songs tell of God's grace to undeserving people, God's victory over the enemy, and the wonderful way God turns things upside down in order to accomplish His purposes. What Mary expressed in her song is especially close to what Hannah sang in her hymn of praise.

The joy of the Lord (1 Sam. 2:1). Hannah was praying and rejoicing at the same time! She was thinking of God's blessing to the nation of Israel as well as to herself and her home. When prayer is selfish it isn't spiritual and it does not honor the Lord. Hannah knew in her heart that God was going to do great things for His people and that her son would play an important part in accomplishing God's will. Her worship came from her heart and was saturated with the joy of the Lord.

The word "horn" in verses 1 and 10 symbolizes strength or a strong person (see Pss. 75:4-5, 10; 89:17, 24; 92:10; 132:17). To have your "horn exalted" meant to receive new strength from God and be especially helped by Him at a time of crisis. An "enlarged mouth" means a mouth boasting of God's victory over His enemies. Defeated people have to keep their mouths shut, but those who share God's victory have something to talk about to the glory of God.

"I rejoice in thy salvation" suggests more than Hannah's being delivered from barrenness. Hannah sees this miracle as the beginning of new victory for Israel who time after time had been invaded, defeated, and abused by their enemies (Jud. 2:10-23). But the word "salvation" is *yeshua*—Joshua—one of the names of the promised Messiah. King David would be God's *yeshua* to deliver Israel from her enemies, and Jesus the Son of David would be God's *yeshua* to deliver all people from the bondage of sin and death.

The majesty of the Lord (1 Sam. 2:2-3). It's good for us to begin our praying with praising, because praise helps us focus on the glory of the Lord and not on the greatness of our needs. When we see the greatness of God, we start to see life in perspective. Hannah knew the character of God and exalted His glorious attributes. She began by affirming His *holiness* and *uniqueness.* The two go together because in both Hebrew and Greek the word "holy" means "wholly other, set apart, separated." Orthodox Jews confess daily, "Hear, O Israel: the Lord our God is one Lord" (Deut. 6:4, KJV). There is no other God, and whenever Israel turned to idols for help, they lost the blessing of the Lord.

The "Rock" is one of the repeated images of the Lord in the Scriptures. It's found in the "Song of Moses" (Deut. 32:4, 15, 18, 30-31, 37) and in David's song (2 Sam. 22:32). The rock speaks of the Lord's strength, stability, and steadfastness and magnifies the fact that He does not change. We can depend on Him, for His character is unchangeable and His promises never fail. "For I am the Lord, I change not" (Mal. 3:6 KJV).

The Lord is also "a God of knowledge" (1 Sam. 2:3), so people had better be careful what they say and how they say it. There's no place for pride and arrogance when you stand before a God who knows you through and through, everything you've thought, spoken, and done. God heard all of Peninnah's haughty words spoken against Hannah, and He also heard Hannah's prayer from her heart. God is omniscient and knows all things, and He is omnipresent and beholds all things.

Hannah rejoiced because this holy God is a *just judge* of the actions of His people. Unlike the people involved in human judicial proceedings, the Lord knows everything and is able to weigh us and our actions accurately. He weighed Belshazzar and found him "wanting" (Dan. 5:27). The Lord weighs our motives (Prov. 16:2) and our hearts (24:11-12), and His scales are accurate. Like Hannah, we may be misunderstood and maligned by people, but the Lord will always act justly.

The grace of the Lord (1 Sam. 2:4-8a). God is holy and just and is always true to His Word and His character. But He is also merciful and gracious and often does things that catch us by surprise. Hannah described some of His acts and affirmed that the Lord turned everything upside down! The "Song of Mary" (The Magnificat) in Luke 1:46-55 expresses some of these same truths.

The mighty warriors fail while the stumbling weaklings win the battle (1 Sam. 2:4; see Ecc. 9:11). The rich people with plenty of food are looking for something to eat and are willing to labor for it, while the poor hungry people have more than they need (1 Sam. 2:5a). The barren woman gives birth to seven children, while the woman with many children is exhausted and feeble and can't even enjoy her family (v. 5b). The truth in this statement is reflected in the fact that Hannah bore five more children (v. 21).

Because He is sovereign, the Lord is in charge of life and death and everything in between (v. 6). He can rescue us from the grave or permit us to die. If He allows us to live, He can make us rich or poor, exalted or abased, for He knows what's best. This doesn't suggest that people should meekly comply with difficult circumstances and do nothing about them, but that we can't change these circumstances without the Lord's help (Deut. 8:18). In His grace, God can choose the poor and raise them up to sit among the princes (see Ps. 113:7-8 and Luke 1:52). He takes them from the dust and the garbage heap and puts them on glorious thrones! But isn't that what God did for Jesus (Phil. 2:1-10) and what Jesus did for us when He saved us? (Eph. 2:1-10) Indeed, because of the cross, the Lord has "turned the world upside down" (Acts 17:6), and the only people who have clear vision and true values are those who have trusted Jesus.

The protection of the Lord (1 Sam. 2:8b-10a). God has established the world so that it can't be moved, and what happens on our planet is under His watchful care.[5] We may think that God has abandoned the earth to Satan and his demonic powers, but this is still our Father's world (Ps. 24:1-2), and He has set His King on heaven's throne (Ps. 2:7-9). As God's people walk on this earth and walk in the light, the Lord will guard and guide their steps, but the wicked will walk in spiritual darkness because they depend on their own wisdom and strength. It may seem that the wicked "have it made," but one day the storm of God's wrath will burst upon them in fierce judgment. God is long-suffering with those who resist Him, but their day is coming.

The reign of the Lord (1 Sam. 2:10b). This is a remarkable statement that the Lord will give an anointed king to Israel and strengthen him to serve Him and the nation. Hannah certainly knew the Law of Moses because in them she found the promises of a future king. God told Abraham and Sarah that kings would come from them (Gen. 17:6, 16), and He repeated this promise to Jacob (35:11). In his last words to his sons, Jacob announced that Judah would be the royal tribe (49:10); and in Deuteronomy 17:14-20, Moses gave instructions concerning a future king. When Israel asked for a king, God was prepared to grant their request. In many respects, King David fulfilled this prophecy; but the ultimate fulfillment is in Jesus the Christ ("Anointed One") who will one day sit on David's throne and rule over His glorious kingdom (Luke 1:32-33, 69-75).

Hannah and Elkanah left their son in Shiloh and returned to Ramah with joyful hearts and great expectation to see what the Lord would do. What a wonderful thing it is when a husband and wife are dedicated to the Lord, worship Him together, pray together, and trust His Word. Hannah went to the place of worship with a broken heart, but the Lord gave her peace because she prayed and submitted to His will.

4. God judges sin (1 Sam. 2:12-36)

Up to this point, the focus has been on Elkanah and his family (1:1–2:11), but now it will shift to Eli and his family (2:12–3:21). Throughout this section, you will see a deliberate contrast between Samuel and the two sons of Eli, Hophni and Phinehas. Eli's sons "abhorred the offering of the Lord" (2:17), but "Samuel ministered before the Lord" (v. 18). The two brothers committed evil deeds at the tabernacle and invited God's judgment, but Samuel served at the tabernacle and grew in God's favor (v. 26). The priestly line would end in Eli's family, but Samuel would be called of God to carry on a holy priesthood (2:34–3:1). From the human viewpoint, it looked as though Eli's evil sons were getting away with their disobedience, but God was preparing judgment for them while He was equipping His servant Samuel to continue His work.

God's judgment deserved (1 Sam. 2:12-21). Since Eli was an old man with failing vision (4:15), he left the work of the tabernacle to his two sons, and they took advantage of their father by doing what they pleased. Hophni and Phinehas did not personally know the Lord but were "sons of Belial," a Hebrew term that described worthless people who openly practiced lawlessness (Deut. 13:13; Jud. 19:22; 1 Sam. 25:25; Prov. 16:27). In 2 Corinthians 6:15, Paul uses Belial as a synonym for Satan. The law stated precisely what portions of the sacrifices belonged to the priests (Lev. 7:28-36; 10:12-15; Deut. 18:1-5), but the two brothers took the meat that they wanted and also took the fat parts that belonged to the Lord. They even took raw meat so they could roast it and not have

23

to eat boiled meat. They "abhorred the offering of the Lord" (1 Sam. 2:17) and "trampled on" (scorned) the Lord's sacrifices (v. 29).

Hophni and Phinehas not only showed disrespect for the sacrifices on the altar, but they also had no regard for the women who served at the door of the tabernacle (v. 22; Ex. 38:8). Instead of encouraging them in their spiritual walk, the two brothers seduced them. These women were not official servants appointed by the law but were volunteers who assisted the priests and Levites. Perhaps they helped care for the little children who came with the adult worshipers, or they may have been there just to be close to the presence of the Lord. Ministerial immorality is in the news today, and it's a tragic thing, but it's really nothing new.

In contrast to the wickedness of Eli's sons is the faithfulness of Samuel (1 Sam. 2:18-21). He was somewhat of an apprentice priest, learning the work of the sanctuary, and even wore a linen robe with an ephod (vest) over it, just as the adult priests and Levites did. Each year when his parents came to Shiloh, his mother would bring a new set of garments for the growing lad. In Scripture, garments often speak of the spiritual life (Isa. 61:10; Zech. 3:1-5; Eph. 4:22-32; Col. 3:8-17; 1 Peter 5:5), and a change of clothing symbolizes a new beginning (Gen. 35:2; 41:14; 45:22; Ex. 19:10; Rev. 3:18). Each year's new garments spoke not only of a boy growing physically but also spiritually (1 Sam. 2:21), and this reminds us of our Lord who "increased in wisdom and stature, and in favor with God and men" (Luke 2:52, NKJV).

God was about to bring judgment to the house of Eli, but the Lord blessed Elkanah and Hannah and their house, for He gave her five more children (1 Sam. 2:21; see Ps. 113:9). This was the gracious gift of God and an answer to the prayer of Eli (1 Sam. 2:20) who was pleased with Samuel and grateful for his ministry. Hannah gave one child to the Lord and the Lord gave back five!

God's judgment disregarded (1 Sam. 2:22-26). Godly people told Eli about his sons' sins, and he spoke to them about their conduct, but it did no good. He wasn't much of a godly father or spiritual leader, and his sons disregarded his warnings. It's tragic when a father—and a spiritual leader at that—loses his influence over his own family and can only wait for God's hand of judgment to fall. Lot lost his influence with his family (Gen. 19:12-14), and after David sinned with Bathsheba, his influence over his sons was greatly weakened. Hophni and Phinehas had no respect for the Lord or for the office of their father the high priest, so all God could do was judge them and replace them with faithful servants.

God's judgment declared (1 Sam. 2:27-36). An anonymous "man of God" appeared at Shiloh to declare the terms of God's judgment on Eli and his family. The title "man of God" is used some seventy times in the Old Testament and usually refers to a prophet sent by the Lord. First, the prophet dealt with *the past* (vv. 27-28) and reminded Eli that his position as high priest was a gift of God's grace. The Lord had chosen Aaron to be the first high priest and given him the privilege of passing this honor on to his eldest son (Ex. 4:14-16; 28:1-4). It was a privilege for the high priest and his sons to offer sacrifices on the brazen altar, burn incense on the golden altar, wear the sacred garments, and eat of the holy offerings. Then the messenger focused on *the present* (1 Sam. 2:29) and accused Eli of putting his sons ahead of the Lord and sharing in their sins. (The "you" at the beginning of v. 29 is plural and includes Eli with his sons.) To tolerate sin and not deal with it severely is to participate in that sin. As high priest, Eli had the authority to discipline his sons, but he refused to do so. "Do not share in the sins of others" (1 Tim. 5:22 NIV). If Eli had been a man of God, concerned for the glory of God, he would have remonstrated with his sons and called them to repent; and if they refused, he would have replaced them.

But the burden of the prophet's message was centered on *the future* (1 Sam. 2:30-36). God had given the priesthood to Aaron and his descendants forever, and nobody could take this honor (Ex. 29:9; 40:15; Num. 18:7; Deut. 18:5). However, God's servants can't live any way they please and expect the Lord to honor them; for "them who honor me I will honor" (1 Sam. 2:30). The privilege of the priesthood would remain with the tribe of Levi and the house of Aaron, but God would take it away from Eli's branch of the family. Eli's descendants would become weak and die off and there would be no more old men like Eli in the family. They would have to beg for their food and would plead for an opportunity to serve (v. 36). In David's day the descendants of Eleazar outnumbered those of Ithamar at least two to one (1 Chron. 24:1-5), so Eli's family did slowly die out. But even worse, very soon Eli's two pampered sons would die on the same day. Even the tabernacle would experience distress (1 Sam. 2:32, NIV), which turned out to include the capture of the ark and ultimately the moving of the tabernacle from Shiloh to Nob (21:1-6; Jer. 7:14). However, at Nob many of the priests were slain by Doeg, which was a partial fulfillment of this prophecy.

Eli descended from Aaron through Ithamar, Aaron's fourth son, but God would abandon that line and turn to the sons of Eleazar, Aaron's third son and successor in the high priesthood.[6] Under David, both Zadok and Abiathar served as high priests (2 Sam. 8:17), but when Solomon became king, he removed Eli's great-great grandson Abiathar from the high priesthood because he had cooperated with David's son Adonijah in his attempt to seize the throne. Solomon appointed Zadok to serve as high priest, and he was of the house of Eleazar. (See 1 Kings 2:26-27, 35.) In the list of Jewish high priests in 1 Chronicles 6:3-15, the names from Eli to Abiathar are missing. By confirming Zadok as high priest, Solomon fulfilled the prophecy given by the man of God nearly a century and a half before.[7]

But the future wasn't all bleak, for the man of God announced that God would raise up a faithful priest who would please God's heart and do God's will (1 Sam. 2:35). The immediate reference is to Zadok, but ultimately it points to Jesus Christ who alone could have a "sure house" and be God's anointed priest "forever." Our Lord came from the tribe of Judah, so He had no connection with the house of Aaron, but was made a high priest after the order of Melchizedek (Heb. 7–8).

5. God rewards faithfulness (1 Sam. 3:1-21)

Once again we see the contrast between the wickedness of Eli's family and the faithfulness of the boy Samuel (v. 1). He ministered before the Lord under the guidance of Eli at a time when God wasn't speaking to His people very often. The spiritual leaders were corrupt, and God's people weren't obeying His law anyway, so why should God say anything new to them? It was a tragic day in the nation of Israel when the living God no longer sent His people signs and prophetic messages (Ps. 74:9; Ezek. 7:26; Amos 8:11-12; Micah 3:6). The silence of God was the judgment of God.

But God was about to change the situation and speak His precious Word to a young boy who would listen and obey.

An attentive ear (1 Sam. 3:1-9). Samuel was probably twelve years old when the Lord spoke to him one night as he lay in the tabernacle "annex" where Eli was also sleeping. The "lamp of God" was the seven-branched golden candlestick that stood in the holy place before the veil, to the left of the golden altar of incense (Ex. 25:31-40; 27:20-21; 37:17-24). It was the only source of light in the holy place, and the priests were ordered to keep it burning always (27:20) and to trim the wicks when they offered the incense each morning and evening (30:7-8). The lamp was a symbol of the light of God's truth given to the world through His people Israel. Alas, the light of God's Word was burning dimly in those days, and God's high priest was barely able to see! The ark was there, containing the law of God (25:10-22; 37:1-9; Heb. 9:1-5), but the law was not honored by God's people.

The Lord spoke to Samuel four times (1 Sam. 3:4, 6, 8, 10), and the first three times, Samuel thought it was Eli calling him. One of the marks of a faithful servant is an attentive ear and an immediate response. But Samuel had never heard God's voice, so he didn't know who was calling to him. Like Saul of Tarsus, Samuel's call and conversion occurred at the same time, except that Samuel's experience was at night while Saul saw a blazing light when he heard God's voice (Acts 9:1-9). Eli was discerning enough to realize that God was speaking to the boy, so he told him how to respond.

An obedient will (1 Sam. 3:10-14). Samuel obeyed Eli, went back to his sleeping place, and waited for the voice to come again. This time God spoke the boy's name twice, for the Shepherd calls His sheep by name and gets their attention (John 10:3, 14).[8] Not only that, the Lord came and stood near Samuel as He spoke to him. This experience wasn't a dream or a vision but a manifestation of the presence of the Lord. Samuel's response was, "Speak, for your servant is listening" (1 Sam. 3:10, NIV), and he left out the word, "Lord" (see v. 9). Why? Samuel didn't yet have a personal knowledge of the Lord (v. 7), so he couldn't know whose voice it was that had spoken to him. Perhaps he was being careful not to accept it as the voice of Jehovah when he had no way to be sure.

Because Samuel was obedient to God and to Eli, he heard the message from the Lord and learned what God planned to do. This was certainly a weighty message to give to a young boy, but in so doing, perhaps God was rebuking the spiritual lethargy of the adults, for to which of them could God give this message? When God can't find an obedient adult, He sometimes calls a child. "And I will make mere lads their princes" (Isa. 3:4, NASB).

Samuel didn't know the message the unknown prophet had delivered to Eli, but the message God gave him confirmed it. The Lord would judge the house of Eli because Eli's two sons "made themselves vile [contemptible]" and Eli did nothing to restrain them. Though Eli and his sons were priests, they could offer no sacrifice that would atone for their sins! Their sins were deliberate and defiant, and for such sins no sacrifice could be offered (Num. 15:30). Not only had they defiled themselves, but they had also defiled the priesthood. The Lord had been long-suffering toward the house of Eli, but they hadn't repented and turned from their sins; now it was too late.

A humble heart (1 Sam. 3:15-18). Samuel had heard the voice of God and received the message of God, but he still got up early and went back to his old tasks. He opened the doors of the sanctuary so the people could come to sacrifice,[9] and he said nothing to Eli about what God had told him. This shows remarkable maturity on the part of a young boy. Most youths would have been proud of their experience with the Lord, rushed around delivering the message, and would not have stooped to open doors. It was only when Eli commanded him that Samuel related the message of judgment that God had given to him.

Was Eli's response to the message active submission or passive resignation to something that couldn't be changed? I vote for resignation, the same attitude that Hezekiah displayed when Isaiah told him his foolish actions would one day bring ruin to the kingdom of Judah (Isa. 39). Eli was an old man who had not been a good father or a faithful priest, and he had already been warned that judgment was coming. His two sons would perish in one day and his family would lose the privilege of the priesthood, so what was there to live for? God had chosen Samuel to be judge, priest, and prophet, so the light of truth would keep burning in Israel. All the old man could do was to wait patiently for the sword to fall.

Eli had his faults as we all do, and we must appreciate his positive attitude toward young Samuel, his successor as the spiritual leader in Israel. It isn't every veteran servant who can graciously lay down his tools and let the young apprentice take over. Until the very end of his life, Eli at least had a concern for the ark of God and the future of the nation; and the news of Israel's defeat and the capture of the ark caused his death. If Eli had shown some of this concern when his sons were young like Samuel, things would have been different.

A godly walk (1 Sam. 3:19-21). For the second time we're told that Samuel grew (2:21; 3:19), but the affirmation is added, "the Lord was with him." This statement will also be made about youthful David (16:18; 18:12, 14). The Lord was against Eli and his sons, but His blessing was upon Samuel and his ministry. Unlike the other judges, Samuel's words and influence would reach the entire nation. The people recognized that God had called Samuel to be a prophet and declare the Word of God and the will of God. Once again, the Lord appeared from time to time at Shiloh and revealed Himself to His prophet. Israel was about to experience a new beginning that would lead to new challenges and dangers as well as new blessings and victories.

TWO

1 SAMUEL 4–6

Israel's Defeat—God's Victory

The ark of the covenant is mentioned at least thirty-five times in these three chapters and represents Jehovah God, the central person in all of Israel's history. The ark was the most important piece of furniture in the tabernacle and resided in the Holy of Holies. In the ark were the two tables of the law, and on it was the golden "mercy seat" where God's glorious presence dwelt. This was the throne of God from which He spoke to His people (Ex. 25:10-22). To the eye of faith, God is very evident and active in all the events recorded in these chapters. None of these events happened by accident; they were all part of God's plan to chasten His people, judge sinners, and eventually establish His anointed king

1. The faithful Word of God (1 Sam. 4:1-22)

No sooner does God begin to reveal His Word to His people than the enemy shows up to attack them. The Philistines are mentioned in Scripture as early as the days of Abraham (Gen. 21:32; see 10:14), and in the Books of Samuel they're mentioned over 150 times. They were originally a seagoing people from the Aegean region who invaded the territory along the

Mediterranean coast (Phoenicia) and sought to control all of the land we know as Palestine. (The name "Palestine" is a form of the word "Philistine.") The Philistines were very distressed when Israel conquered the Promised Land and many times attempted to drive them out. It's likely that this particular battle was Israel's response to one of those Philistine invasions.

Israel was defeated (1 Sam. 4:1-10). Aphek was a northern Philistine city about three miles west of the Jewish city of Ebenezer ("stone of help").[1] Shiloh lay about twenty miles east of Ebenezer. In their initial confrontation, the Philistines defeated Israel and killed 4,000 men, and the elders of Israel were perplexed over this defeat. Wasn't Israel God's chosen nation, and didn't He give them the land as their possession? Then why was Israel defeated by their idol-worshiping neighbors? If the elders had recalled the terms of God's covenant, they would have realized that this shameful defeat was caused by Israel's disobedience to God's law (Lev. 26:39; Deut. 28:25).

The Lord had clearly told them how to fight their wars (Deut. 20), but instead of searching their hearts and confessing their sins, the people decided to imitate Moses and Joshua and take the ark of the covenant into the battle with them. (See Num. 10:33-36; Josh. 3–4 and 6.) But this approach was merely "using God" to accomplish their own purposes. Unlike Moses and Joshua, they didn't seek the will of the Lord, they weren't walking by faith, and they certainly weren't seeking to glorify God. Even worse, the two wicked priests Hophni and Phinehas would be carrying the holy ark of God! How could God bless two sinful men whom He had already consigned to judgment? (1 Sam. 2:29, 34–4:4,17) But Israel's hope was that the presence of the ark would save the Jews from the hand of their enemies.[2]

When Hophni and Phinehas appeared in the camp carrying the ark of God, the soldiers and elders shouted enthusiastically, but their carnal self-confidence was just the prelude to another defeat. The ark may have been with them in the camp, but the Lord was against them. Their joyful shout may have bolstered their spirits, but it was no guarantee of victory. All it did was motivate the Philistine army to determine to fight harder and win the battle, which they did, killing 30,000 Jewish soldiers. God will not be "used" just to make sinful people achieve their own selfish purposes. God's promise is, "Them who honor me I will honor" (2:30).

The ark was taken (1 Sam. 4:11a). Five times in verses 11-22 you find the phrase "the ark of God was [is] taken" (vv. 11, 17, 19, 21-22). Never in the history of Israel had the ark of God ever fallen into enemy hands! So holy was the ark that it was kept behind the veil in the tabernacle and seen only by the high priest on the annual Day of Atonement (Lev. 16). When the Jewish camp moved during the nation's years of wandering, the first thing the high priest did was cover the ark with the veil (Num. 4:5-6), and only then would he attend to the other pieces of furniture.

The ark of God was the throne of God (2 Sam. 6:2, NIV; also Pss. 80:1 and 99:1), but now God's throne was in enemy territory! The Jews had forgotten that the ark was God's throne in Israel *only if Israel was submitted to Him and obedient to His covenant.* Anything else was nothing but ignorant superstition, like people trusting good-luck charms. It wasn't a sin to take the ark into battle if the people were truly devoted to the Lord and wanted to honor Him. God put the ark into pagan hands, but Eli's two sons had lived like pagans while ministering before the ark, so what was the difference? God would use the ark to teach both the Jews and the Philistines some important lessons.

The two priests were slain (1 Sam. 4;11b). This fulfilled the Word of God spoken to Eli by the anonymous prophet (2:27-36) and to Samuel when he was called by the Lord (3:11-18). God had been long-suffering with Hophni and Phinehas as they desecrated His sacrifices and defiled His people, but now their time was up and their sins had found them out.

The high priest died (1 Sam. 4:12-18). Eli knew that his sons had entered the Holy of Holies and taken the ark to the battlefield, but he was unable to stop them, just as he had been unable to control them in past years. He wasn't worrying about his sons as he sat in his special seat by the tabernacle; he was trembling for the safety of the ark of God. But didn't Eli realize that God was still on the heavenly throne even if His earthly throne had been cheapened and transformed into a good-luck charm? Wasn't the Lord able to protect His own furniture and His own glory?

The messenger ran first to the busiest part of Shiloh and delivered the sad news of Israel's defeat, and the people's loud lamenting caught Eli's attention. The messenger ran to Eli to gave him the bad news: Israel was defeated, there was a great slaughter, Hophni and Phinehas were both slain and—as if saving the worst news for the last—the ark of God had been taken by the Philistines. Eli must have suffered a stroke or a heart attack, for he fell back, broke his neck, and died. He was "a heavy man,"[3] probably caused by eating too much meat from the sacrifices (2:29) and leading a sedentary life. The death of Eli and his two sons was the beginning of the fulfillment of God's prophecy that Eli's branch of the priesthood would be destroyed and a new line introduced.

The glory of God departed (1 Sam. 4:19-22). The wife of Phinehas had more spiritual insight than her father-in-law, her husband, and her brother-in-law. The two brothers used the ark as a good luck charm, Eli was concerned with the safety of the ark, but she was burdened for the glory of God. She named her son Ichabod—"the glory is gone"—and then she died.[4] The presence of God's glory in the camp was a special sign that the Israelites were the people of God (Ex. 40:34; Rom. 9:4), but now the glory had departed and God's special favor was gone. When King Solomon dedicated the temple, the glory of God returned (1 Kings 8:10), but before the destruction of Jerusalem, the Prophet Ezekiel saw the glory leave the temple and the city (Ezek. 8:4; 9:3; 10:4, 18; 11:22-23). Ezekiel also saw the future millennial temple and the return of the glory of God (Ezek. 43:1-5). The glory of God didn't return to this earth until the birth of Jesus Christ, the Savior of the world (Luke 2:8-11; John 1:14). Today, God's glory dwells in His people individually (1 Cor. 6:19-

20) and in His church collectively (Eph. 2:19-22).

So significant was this tragic event that Asaph the psalmist included it in one of his psalms (Ps. 78:60-61). But he tells us that much more happened than the capture of the ark by the Philistines, for the Lord abandoned the tabernacle at Shiloh and allowed the enemy to destroy it (Jer. 7:12-14; 26:6, 9). The Philistines eventually returned the ark and it remained first in Beth-shemesh and then Kiriath-jearim (1 Sam. 6:13-21). The priests must have constructed some kind of tabernacle at Nob (1 Sam. 21:1ff), but in Solomon's day, it was at Gibeon (1 Chron. 21:29; 1 Kings 3:4). Eventually Solomon incorporated the tabernacle into the temple which he built (2 Chron. 5:5).

The wicked sons of Eli thought their scheme would save the glory of God, but it only took the glory of God away!

2. The vindicating power of God (1 Sam. 5:1-12)

The five key cities of the Philistines were Ashdod, Gaza, Ashkelon, Gath, and Ekron, and each had a ruler or "lord" (6:16-17). The Philistines first put the ark into the temple of their god Dagon in Ashdod as evidence that Dagon was stronger and greater than Jehovah. At the beginning of the battle, the Philistines were frightened when they heard that the God of Israel was in the camp, but now they were making fun of Him and exalting their own gods. In their mythology, Dagon was the principal god of the Philistines and the father of Baal, the storm god, whose worship brought so much trouble to Israel.

However, Dagon didn't have a chance, for Jehovah God was and is well able to take care of Himself! The next morning, the worshipers found Dagon prostrate before the ark like one of the worshipers. Like every dead idol, Dagon had to be righted again (Ps. 115), but things were even worse the next morning. The stump of Dagon was prostrate before the ark of the covenant, but his head and hands had been cut off and placed at the threshold of the temple! But that wasn't the end, for the Lord not only humiliated the god of the Philistines, but he judged the people who worshiped that god. When the Philistines captured the ark and arrogantly treated the Lord as though He were just another god, they invited the judgment of God.

When you put the evidence together, it seems that the Lord sent infected mice or rats (1 Sam. 6:4) among the people and spread a terrible plague. According to the covenant, the Lord should have sent this affliction on the unbelieving Jews (Deut. 28:58-60), but in His grace, He punished the enemy. Some students believe this was the bubonic plague and that the people experienced painful inflammatory swellings of the lymph glands, especially in the groin. Others think it was a plague of tumors, perhaps severe hemorrhoids (see 1 Sam. 5:9), although it's difficult to understand the part the rats played in this affliction. Whatever the punishment was, it pained and humiliated the Philistines who attributed their suffering to the presence of the ark.

But the five lords of the Philistines were anxious to preserve the glory of their victory. If they could prove that the calamity was a coincidence, they could retain the ark and continue to magnify Dagon's superiority over Jehovah. The easiest way to do this was to move the ark to another city and see what happened, so they took it to Gath—and the same thing happened! Then they carried it to Ekron, where the people protested and told them to take it elsewhere! God killed a number of citizens ("deadly destruction") and also sent a painful plague to the people of Ekron just as He had done to the inhabitants of Ashdod and Gath. God had vindicated Himself and proved that it was His hand that had destroyed the statue of Dagon and that brought affliction to the Philistine people. Nobody could call the eruption of these plagues a mere coincidence. But the lords of the Philistines still had to figure out how to get rid of the ark without humiliating themselves and perhaps bringing more judgment on their land.

3. The wise providence of God (1 Sam. 6:1-18)
The experiences described in 5:1-12 occurred during a period of seven months, at the end of which the five lords decided it was

time to get rid of the ark. They wouldn't admit it, but Jehovah had vindicated Himself before the Philistines and humiliated their false god. Still wanting to save face, the lords sought some way to send the ark back to Israel without directly involving themselves or their people.

Man proposes (1 Sam. 6:1-9). The Philistine wise men came up with a scheme that would test the God of Israel one more time. If Jehovah, represented by the ark, was indeed the true and living God, *let Him take the ark back to where it belonged!* The lords set up a plan that would absolve them of responsibility and blame. They would take two cows that had calves and separate them from the calves. They would hitch the cows to a new cart, put the ark on the cart, and turn the cows loose. If the cows didn't move at all, or if they went to their calves, it would be "proof" that the God of Israel wasn't in control and the Philistines had nothing to fear. If the cows meandered all over without any sense of direction, the lords could draw the same conclusion. The situation being what it was, the cows would probably head for their calves, because that was the natural thing to do. The cows needed to get rid of their milk and the calves needed the nourishment.

But that wasn't all. The wise men decided that the nation had to send "appeasement gifts" to Jehovah in the form of golden models of the mice and the tumors. If the cows didn't head for Israelite territory, the Philistines could always reclaim their gold. If the cows went over the border into Israel, the Lord would be appeased and wouldn't send Philistia any more plagues. This plan enabled the Lord to receive glory without the lords of the Philistines being embarrassed. When you consider that the cows were nursing their calves and lowing for them, and that the cows had never drawn a cart before, the odds were that they wouldn't go down the road that led from Ekron to Beth-Shemesh. The five lords and their wise men had it all figured out.

God disposes (1 Sam. 6:10-18). But they were wrong. The lords of the Philistines didn't know the true and living God, but the cows did, and they obeyed Him! "The ox knows its owner and the donkey its master's crib" (Isa. 1:3, NKJV). They crossed the border and came to the priestly city of Beth-Shemesh (Josh. 21:13-16) where the men were working in the fields harvesting the wheat. They joyfully welcomed the return of the ark, and the Levites took it off the cart and put it on a great stone in the field.

Grateful that the throne of God had been restored to His people, the Levites offered the cows as burnt offerings to the Lord, and in their joy ignored the fact that only male animals could legally be offered (Lev. 1:3). Other men from the city brought additional sacrifices. They also put the golden gifts on the rock and offered them to the Lord. Since Shiloh had been destroyed and there was no sanctuary available for worship, they used the large rock as an altar, and the Lord accepted their offerings. What the Lord is looking for is a broken and contrite heart, not a slavish obedience to the letter of the law (Ps. 51:15-17). The enemy was near at hand (1 Sam. 6:16) and the Jewish men didn't dare leave the place to which God had directed the cows.

God had done what Dagon could never do: He guided the cows, kept their attention on the right road, overcame their desire to go to their calves, and brought them to the priestly city of Beth-Shemesh. His providence rules over all. Alas, the priests and Levites didn't do their job well, and what should have been a great cause for joy turned out to be a cause of sorrow because of man's foolishness. Eventually the ark would be given a safe resting place until King David would move it to a specially prepared place in Jerusalem (2 Sam. 6:12ff).

4. The holy wrath of God (1 Sam. 6:19-20)
The men of Beth-Shemesh should have covered the ark, because it wasn't supposed to be seen by anyone except the high priest, and this mistake was costly. Some of the people became curious and looked into the ark and were slain. If the pagan Philistines were judged for the way they treated the ark, how much more responsible were the Jews who knew the law and were living in a levitical city!

Students have debated the accuracy of the number of people who were killed, because 50,000 seems too high for a town like

Beth-Shemesh. Some make the number only 70 and say that the 50,000 is a scribal error, and perhaps it is. The Hebrews used letters for numbers and it would be easy for a copyist to make a mistake. Others include in the 50,000 the 4,000 plus "the great slaughter" (4:17) on the battlefield, but the text specifically says it was the irreverent people who looked into the ark who were slain. (See 1 Sam. 6:19; Lev. 16:13; Num. 1:50-51; 4:5, 16-20.) It isn't likely that 50,000 people lined up and passed by the ark, for the people queued up would have scattered when the first viewers were killed. Perhaps they were slain later. Certainly the Levites would have protected the ark from the curious, for they knew the penalties for breaking the law of God. That 70 men were judged isn't difficult to believe, but 50,000 seems extravagant. However, since we don't know the population of Beth-Shemesh and its environs, we can't pass judgment on the text. One day an archeologist may solve the problem for us.

While God doesn't live in our church buildings or in any of its furnishings (Acts 7:48-50), we do want to show respect for anything dedicated to the the glory of God. The awesome event described here certainly warns us against religious curiosity and lack of reverence for the Lord. "It is a fearful thing to fall into the hands of the living God" (Heb. 10:31, KJV). In today's Western society, with its informality and lack of respect for the sacred, it's easy even for believers to get so "chummy" with the Lord that they forget He is "high and lifted up."

5. The merciful grace of God (1 Sam. 6:21–7:2)

The Lord could have withdrawn Himself from His people, but instead, He graciously allowed the ark to be taken about ten miles to Kiriath Jearim where it remained in the home of Abinadab. The men of the city consecrated Abinadab's son Eleazar to guard the ark. This was undoubtedly a levitical family, for after what had happened to the men of Beth-Shemesh, the men weren't likely to take any more chances by breaking the law! The ark remained in Kiriath Jearim for perhaps a century, for the battle of Aphek was fought about 1104 B.C., and David brought the ark to Jerusalem in about 1003 B.C. (2 Sam. 6). The ark had been in the home of Abinadab twenty years when Samuel called an assembly of the people to turn from their sins and seek the Lord (1 Sam. 7:3).

The ark of the covenant represented the presence of the Lord with His people and the rule of the Lord over His people. The Lord had every right to abandon His sinful people, but He graciously remained with them, though not in the special tabernacle He had commanded them to build. It was a difficult time for the Jews, for they were not a united people, nor were they a godly people. Israel thought that their problems would be solved if they had a king like the other nations, but they would discover that having their own way would lead them into greater problems. God still gives His best to those who leave the choice with Him.

What the ark was to Israel, Jesus Christ is to God's people today; and when He is given His rightful place of preeminence in our lives, He will bless us and work on our behalf. "But in your hearts set apart Christ as Lord," is the way Peter explained it (1 Peter 3:15, NIV). When Jesus Christ is Lord, the future is your friend, and you can walk through each day confident of His presence and His help.

THREE

1 SAMUEL 17–11

The Call for a King

The ark of the covenant was now out of enemy hands and resting in the house of Abinadab in Kiriath Jearim in the territory of Benjamin (1 Sam. 1-2; Josh. 18:28). Shiloh had been destroyed by the Philistines and was no longer the location of the sanctuary of the Lord, and many years would pass before the ark would be moved to Jerusalem by King David (1 Chron. 15). But having the ark in Jewish territory didn't automatically solve Israel's problems, for during those twenty years when the ark was in Abinidab's house, a new generation had arisen and was crying out for radical changes in Israel's government. For centuries, the people of Israel had looked to Jehovah as their King, but now they asked the Lord to give them a king just like the other nations. It was a critical time in the history of Israel, and it took the prayers and guidance of Samuel to bring them safely through this dangerous time of transition.

1. Seeking the Lord (1 Sam. 7:3-17)
Samuel discerned that the people were restless and wanting change, and he knew that times of transition bring out either the best or the worst in people. God called Samuel to build a bridge

41

between the turbulent age of the Judges and the new era of the monarchy, and it wasn't an easy task. There was one thing Samuel knew for certain: king or no king, the nation could never succeed if the people didn't put the Lord first and trust only in Him. That's why he called for a meeting at Mizpah, a city in Benjamin (Josh. 18:26), where he challenged God's covenant people to return to the Lord.

They put away their false gods (1 Sam. 7:3-4). Idolatry had been Israel's besetting sin. Jacob's family carried false gods with them (Gen. 35:2), and when the Jews were slaves in Egypt, they adopted the gods and goddesses of the Egyptians, and after the Exodus, worshiped some of these idols during the wilderness journeys (Acts 7:42-43). Moses commanded Israel to destroy every evidence of Canaanite religion, but the people eventually lapsed back into idolatry and worshiped the gods of the defeated enemy. Samuel specifically mentioned the Baals and Ashtoreths (1 Sam. 7:3-4). Baal was the Canaanite storm god to whom the Jews often turned when the land was suffering drought, and Ashtoreth was the goddess of fertility whose worship included unspeakably sensual activities. At Mount Sinai, the Jews didn't see a representation of God, but they heard His voice; and they knew that worshiping any image of their God was to practice false worship.

But putting away their false gods was only the beginning of their return to the Lord; the Jews also had to prepare their hearts for the Lord and devote themselves to the Lord alone (v. 3). This was in keeping with the first commandment, "You shall have no other gods before me" (Ex. 20:3, NIV). An idol is a substitute for God, anything that we trust and serve in place of the Lord. The Jews gave themselves to idols of wood, stone, and metal, but believers today have more subtle and attractive gods: houses and lands, wealth, automobiles, boats, position and recognition, ambition, and even other people. Anything in our lives that takes the place of God and commands the sacrifice and devotion that belong only to Him, is an idol and must be cast out. Idols in the heart are far more dangerous than idols in the temple.

They confessed their sins (1 Sam. 7:5-6). Samuel planned to lead the people in a time of worship and intercession for deliverance from their enemies, but if they had iniquity in their hearts, the Lord would not hear them (Ps. 66:18). It wasn't enough just to destroy their idols; the people also had to confess their sins and surrender themselves to the Lord. Two considerations suggest that this meeting occurred during the time of the Feast of Tabernacles. First, the people poured out water before the Lord, which became a practice at the Feast of Tabernacles, commemorating the times the Lord provided water in the wilderness (John 7:37-39). Second, the people fasted, and this was required only on the annual Day of Atonement, which preceded the Feast of Tabernacles.[1]

The key activity that day was their confession, "We have sinned against the Lord." God's covenant promise to Israel was that He would forgive their sins if they sincerely confessed them to Him (Lev. 26:40-45), for no amount of sacrifices or rituals could wash away their sins. "The sacrifices of God are a broken spirit, a broken and a contrite heart—these, O God, you will not despise" (Ps. 51:17, NKJV). Later in Israel's history, this promise of forgiveness and blessing was reiterated by Solomon at the dedication of the temple (2 Chron. 7:14).

They prayed for God's help (1 Sam. 7:7-11, 13-14). When the Philistines learned about this large gathering of Jews, they became suspicious that Israel was planning to attack, so the five Philistine lords summoned their troops and prepared to invade. Israel had no standing army and no one ruler to organize one, so they felt helpless. But their greatest weapon was their faith in Jehovah God, a faith that was expressed in prayer. "Some trust in chariots, and some in horses, but we will remember the name of the Lord our God" (Ps. 20:7, KJV). As we have seen, Samuel was a man of prayer (99:6), and God answered him that day. As he sacrificed the evening burnt offering, the Lord thundered against the Philistine soldiers and so confused them that it was easy for Israel to attack and defeat them. When we remember that Baal was the Canaanite storm god, it makes the power of God's thunder even more significant.

All the days of Samuel, the Lord kept the Philistines at a distance from Israel. Because of this victory, the Jews recovered cities they had lost in battle and even gained the Amorites as allies. Whenever God's people depend on their own plans and resources, their efforts fail and bring disgrace to God's name; but when God's people trust the Lord and pray, He meets the need and receives the glory. A man or woman of prayer is more powerful than a whole army! No wonder King Jehoash called the Prophet Elisha "the chariots and horsemen of Israel" (2 Kings 13:14), a title Elisha had used for his mentor Elijah (2 Kings 2:12 and see 6:17). Do we have such men and women of prayer today?

They commemorated the victory (1 Sam. 7:12). The setting up of stones to commemorate significant events has been a part of the Hebrew culture since Jacob set up a memorial at Bethel (Gen. 28:20-22; 35:14). Joshua set up twelve stones in the midst of the Jordan (Josh. 4:9) and twelve more on the western bank at Gilgal to mark the place where the waters opened and Israel crossed into the Promised Land (vv. 4:1-8, 19-21). A great heap of stones in the Achor Valley reminded the Jews of Achan's disobedience (vv. 7:24-26), and another heap marked the burial place of the king of Ai (8:29). Another heap stood at a cave at Makkedah to mark where five kings had been defeated and slain (10:25-27). Before his death, Joshua set up a "witness stone" to remind the Israelites of their vow to serve the Lord alone and obey Him (24:26-28).

"Ebenezer" means "stone of help" because the monument was a reminder to the Jews that God had helped them that far and would continue to help them if they would trust Him and keep His covenant. The founder of the China Inland Mission, J. Hudson Taylor, had a plaque displayed in each of his residences that read "Ebenezer—Jehovah Jireh," Together, these Hebrew words say, "The Lord has helped us to this point, and He will see to it from now on." What an encouragement to our faith!

They respected Samuel (1 Sam. 7:15-17). It's likely that this meeting at Mizpah marked the beginning of Samuel's public ministry to the whole nation of Israel, so that from that time on he was a focal point for political unity and spiritual authority. The nation knew that Samuel was God's appointed leader (3:20–4:1), and when he died, the entire nation mourned him (28:3). He made his home in Ramah and established a circuit of ministry to teach the people the law, to hear cases, to give counsel, and to pass judgment. His two sons assisted him by serving at Beersheba (8:1-2). Israel was blessed to have a man like Samuel to guide them, but the times were changing and Israel's elders wanted the nation to change as well.

2. Rejecting the Lord (1 Sam. 8:1-22)

Probably twenty or twenty-five years elapsed between the events recorded in chapter 7 and those in chapter 8. Samuel now an old man, about to pass from the scene, and a new generation had emerged in Israel with new leaders who had new ideas. Life goes on, circumstances change, and God's people must have wisdom to adapt to new challenges without abandoning old convictions. Like more than one great leader, Samuel in his old age faced some painful situations and had to make some difficult decisions. He left the scene convinced that he had been rejected by the people he had served so faithfully. Samuel obeyed the Lord, but he was a man with a broken heart.

God had chosen Moses to lead the nation of Israel and Joshua to succeed him (Deut. 31:1-15), but Joshua wasn't commanded to lay hands on any successor. He left behind elders whom he had trained to serve God, but when they died, the new generation turned away from the Lord and followed the idols of the land (Jud. 2:10-15). There was an automatic succession to the priesthood, and the Lord could call out prophets when needed, but who would lead the people and see to it that the law was obeyed? During the period of the Judges, God raised up leaders here and there and gave them great victories, but nobody was in charge of the nation as a whole. "In those days there was no king in Israel; every man did that which was right in his own eyes" (Jud. 21:25; see 17:6; 18:1; 19:1). The "nation" of Israel was a loose confederation of sovereign tribes, and each tribe was expected to seek the Lord and do His will.

Asking for a king (1 Sam.8:1-9). Knowing that Israel needed a stronger central government, the elders presented their request to Samuel and backed it up with several arguments. The first two must have cut Samuel to the quick: he was now old and had no successor, and his two sons were not godly men but took bribes (1 Sam. 8:3-5). How tragic that both Eli and Samuel had sons who failed to follow the Lord. Eli was too easy on his wayward sons (2:29), and perhaps Samuel was away from home too much as he made his ministry circuit to the cities. Samuel's sons were miles away in Beersheba where their father couldn't monitor their work, but if the elders knew about their sins, surely their father must have known also.

When the elders asked to have a king "like all the nations" (8:5, 20), they were forgetting that Israel's strength was to be *unlike* the other nations. The Israelites were God's covenant people and He was their King. The glory of God dwelt in their midst and the law of God was their wisdom. (See Ex. 19:3-6; 33:15-16; Lev. 18:30 and 20:26; Num. 23:9.) But the elders were concerned about national security and protection from the enemies around them. The Philistines were still a powerful nation, and the Ammonites were also a threat (1 Sam. 12:12). Israel had no standing army and no king to lead it. The elders forgot that it was the Lord who was Israel's King and who gave her army the ability to defeat the enemy.

Samuel was a man of spiritual insight and he knew that this demand for a king was evidence of spiritual decay among the leaders. They weren't rejecting *him*; they were rejecting God, and this grieved Samuel's heart as he prayed to the Lord for wisdom. This wasn't the first time the people had rejected their Lord. At Sinai, their request was "Make us gods!" (Ex. 32:1) and after their humiliating failure at Kadesh Barnea, they said, "Let us make a captain, and let us return into Egypt" (Num. 14:4).[2] Whenever leadership in a church decays spiritually, that church becomes more like the world and uses the world's methods and resources to try to do God's work. The Jewish leaders in Samuel's day had no faith that God could defeat their enemies and protect His people, so they chose to lean on the arm of flesh.

God is never surprised by what His people do, nor is He at a loss to know what He should do. "The Lord brings the counsel of the nations to nothing; He makes the plans of the peoples of no effect. The counsel of the Lord stands forever, the plans of His heart to all generations" (Ps. 33:10-11, NKJV). There is every evidence in the Pentateuch that Israel would one day have a king. God promised Abraham, Sarah, and Jacob that kings would be among their descendants (Gen. 17:6, 16; 35:11), and Jacob had named Judah as the kingly tribe (49:10). Moses prepared the nation for a king when he spoke to the new generation preparing to enter the Promised Land (Deut. 17:14-20).

It wasn't Israel's request for a king that was their greatest sin; it was their insisting that God give them a king immediately. The Lord had a king in mind for them, David the son of Jesse, but the time wasn't ripe for him to appear. So, the Lord gave them their request by appointing Saul to be king, and He used Saul to chasten the nation and prepare them for David, the man of His choice. The fact that Saul was from the tribe of Benjamin and not from Judah is evidence enough that he was never expected to establish a dynasty in Israel. "So in my anger I gave you a king, and in my wrath I took him away" (Hosea 13:11, NIV). The greatest judgment God can give us is to let us have our own way. "And He gave them their request, but sent leanness into their soul" (Ps. 106:15, NKJV). However, the Lord wanted His people to go into this new venture with their eyes open, so He commanded Samuel to tell them what it would cost them to have a king.

Paying for a king (1 Sam. 8:10-22). What's true of individuals is true of nations: you take what you want from life and you pay for it. Under the kingship of Jehovah God, the nation had security and sufficiency as long as they obeyed Him, and His demands were not unreasonable. To obey God's covenant meant to live a happy life as the Lord gave you all that you needed and more. But the key word in Samuel's speech is *take*, not give. The king and his court had to be supported, so he would take their sons and daughters, their property, their harvests, and their flocks and herds. Their choice young men would serve in the army as well as in the king's fields. Their daughters would cook and bake for the king. He would take their property and part of their harvest in order to feed the officials and servants in the royal household. While these things weren't too evident under Saul and David, they were certainly obvious under Solomon (1 Kings 4:7-28). The day came when the people cried out for relief from the heavy yoke Solomon had put on them just to maintain the glory of his kingdom (12:1-4; see Jer. 22:13-17).

In spite of these warnings, the people insisted that God give them a king. Pleasing the Lord wasn't the thing uppermost in their minds; what they wanted was guaranteed protection against their enemies. They wanted someone to judge them and fight their battles, someone they could see and follow. They found it too demanding to trust an invisible God and obey His wonderful commandments. In spite of all the Lord had done for Israel from the call of Abraham to the conquest of the Promised Land, they turned their back on Almighty God and chose to have a frail man to rule over them.

3. Obeying the Lord (1 Sam. 9:1–10:27)

The focus now shifts from Samuel to Saul, God's choice for Israel's king. He was from the tribe of Benjamin, which had almost been exterminated because of their rebellion against the law (Jud. 19–20). Jacob compared Benjamin to "a ravening wolf" (Gen. 49:27), and the tribe was involved in numerous battles. Benjamin's territory lay between Ephraim and Judah, so Saul's tribe was adjacent to the royal tribe of Judah. In spite of what Saul said to Samuel in 1 Samuel 9:21, he belonged to a powerful and wealthy family that owned real estate and animals and had servants.

Physically, Saul was tall, good-looking, and strong, the kind of king people would admire. Even Samuel, with all his spiritual perception, got carried away when he saw him (10:23-24). His weakness for admiring the physical qualities even showed up when

Samuel went to anoint David (16:1-7). Saul was obedient to his father and concerned about his father's feelings (9:5), and he was persistent in wanting to obey his father's will. To invest all that time and energy looking for the lost animals suggests that he wasn't a quitter. There was a certain amount of modesty in Saul (v. 21; 10:14-16), but there was no indication of spiritual life.

Samuel meets Saul (1 Sam. 9:1-25). Saul's home was in Gibeah, which was about five miles from Ramah where Samuel lived, and yet Saul didn't even know what all Israel knew (3:20), that a man of God named Samuel lived in Ramah (9:6). How Saul could live so close to Israel's spiritual leader and not know about him is a bit of a mystery and suggests that Saul simply lived and farmed with his family at Gibeah and minded his own business. Apparently he didn't attend the annual feasts and wasn't greatly concerned about spiritual matters. Like many people today, he wasn't against religion, but he didn't make knowing the Lord a vital part of his life. It's a good thing the servant knew about Samuel and that Saul heeded his advice!

A rather insignificant event brought Saul and Samuel together—the loss of some of Kish's donkeys. The animals were valuable, of course, and later somebody found them and returned them to Kish (10:2), but who would have thought that Israel's first king would be called to the throne while searching for donkeys! David was identified with sheep (Ps. 78:70-72; 1 Sam. 17:15) and saw the people of Israel as sheep who needed protection and guidance (2 Sam. 24:17). The Lord works in unusual ways, but if Saul had not obeyed his father and listened to his servant, the story might have been different.

It was evening when the two men arrived at the gates of Ramah, because the young ladies were going out to draw water. Asking the girls if the seer was there, they were given a long detailed answer. Perhaps the Jewish maids were happy to chat with a tall, handsome stranger! Even the time of Saul's arrival at the city was providential, for Samuel appeared just as Saul and his servant entered the city. Samuel was going up to a "high place" outside the city where he would offer a sacrifice to the

Lord. Since there was no central sanctuary in Israel at that time, the people brought their sacrifices to a shrine that was dedicated to the Lord and located on a hill near the city. The pagan nations worshiped their false gods at the high places and also indulged in filthy practices there, but the people of Israel were forbidden to join them (Ps. 78:58; Hosea 4:11-14; Jer. 3:2).

The day before, the Lord had told Samuel that Saul was coming to Ramah, so he was prepared to meet him and give him God's message. Samuel couldn't say he was happy about the changes going on in Israel, but he was obedient to the Lord. The word "captain" in 1 Samuel 9:16 (KJV) simply means "leader." When Saul appeared, the Lord spoke again to Samuel and confirmed that this was indeed the man of His choice and that Samuel should anoint him as king. "God's anointed" was one of the titles for the king (12:3; 24:6; 26:9, 11, 16; Ps. 2:2, 6). The Lord would use Saul as He did Samson (Jud. 13:5), to begin to weaken the Philistines and prepare them for David's final conquest of this enemy of the Jews (1 Chron. 18:1).

Samuel's response to Saul's request must have shocked the young man. Saul discovered that he was speaking to the man he was seeking, that he would feast with him that day, that Samuel had a special message for him, and that the missing donkeys had been found and returned to his father. Furthermore, all the desire of Israel was fixed on Saul, because all Israel wanted a king. Saul didn't understand what Samuel was saying, but everything would be explained to him the next day. Samuel ignored Saul's protest that he was a nobody who belonged to an insignificant tribe, and he escorted Saul and his servant to the banquet hall at the high place where the feast would be held. Saul was given the special portion of the fellowship offering that belonged to the priest (1 Sam.9:24; Lev. 7:32-33), and the cook informed him that the portion had been set aside especially for him. Strange things were happening! After the feast, Saul returned with Samuel to his house, and there they had a long talk in which Samuel rehearsed for Saul the events that had led up to this meeting.

Samuel anoints Saul (1 Sam. 9:26–10:16). Early the next morning, Samuel accompanied Saul and his servant to the edge of the city, sent the servant on ahead, and then anointed Saul as the first king of Israel. From that moment on, Saul was leader over God's people ("inheritance"), but only Samuel and Saul knew it. How could young Saul be sure that God had really chosen him? Samuel gave Saul three signs, special occurrences he would encounter as he made his way home.

First, he would meet two men who would tell him that the lost animals had been found (10:2), news that Saul had already heard from Samuel. Apparently these men knew who Saul was and that he had been away from home seeking the lost property. But this was a good experience for the young king, for it assured him that *God could solve his problems*. One of Saul's greatest failures as a leader was his inability to take his hands off of situations and let God work. In modern language, Saul was a "control freak." Yet while Saul and his servant were dining with Samuel, God was at work saving the lost animals.

The second sign would take place at the oak of Tabor where he would meet three pilgrims heading for Bethel (vv. 3-4). In spite of the nation's unbelief, there were still devoted people in the land who honored the Lord and sought His face.[3] There must have been a sacred place at Bethel dedicated to the Lord (Jud. 20:18, 26), and perhaps the three kids, the wine, and the three loaves of bread were gifts for the Levites serving there. Since as yet there was no central sanctuary, the three kids may have been for sacrifices. These men would greet Saul and give him two of the three loaves, and he was to receive them. God was showing Saul that not only could He solve his problems, but *He could also supply his needs*. As the first king of Israel, he would have to raise up an army and provide the food and equipment the men needed, and he would have to depend on the Lord.

The third sign had to do with spiritual power (1 Sam. 10:5-6). Saul would meet a band of prophets returning from worship at the high place, and they would be prophesying. The Holy Spirit of God would come upon Saul at that time and he would join the company of prophets in their ecstatic worship. In this sign, God told Saul that *He could endue him with the power he needed for service.* "And who is sufficient for these things?" is the question in the heart of every servant of God (2 Cor. 2:16), and the only correct answer is "our sufficiency is of God" (3:5). However, later Saul would become very self-sufficient and rebellious, and the Lord would take the Spirit from him (1 Sam. 16:14; 28:15).

When Saul turned from Samuel to start his journey home, God gave him "another heart" (10:9, see v. 6). Don't read New Testament "regeneration" into this statement; it refers primarily to a different attitude and outlook. This young farmer would now think and act like a leader, the king of the nation, a warrior-statesman whose responsibility it was to listen to God and obey His will. The Holy Spirit would further enable him to serve God as long as he walked in obedience to His will (v. 6). Because Saul became proud and independent and rebelled against God, he lost the Spirit's power, he lost his kingdom, and he eventually lost his life.

Each of these events took place just as Samuel promised. but the only one actually described in the text is Saul's encounter with the company of prophets (vv. 10-13). In the Old Testament era, God gave His Holy Spirit to chosen people to enable them to perform special tasks, and God could take the Spirit away as well. Believers today, who are under the New Covenant, have the Holy Spirit abiding within forever (John 14:16-17) as God's seal that we are His children (Eph. 1:13-14). When David asked God not to take the Holy Spirit from him (Ps. 51:11), he was thinking especially of what the Lord did to Saul (1 Sam. 16:14; 28:15). Believers today may grieve the Spirit (Eph. 4:30) and quench the Spirit (1 Thes. 5:19), but they cannot drive Him away.

The Spirit enabled Saul (probably for the first time in his life) to have a personal experience with the Lord and to express it in praise and worship. Had Saul continued to nurture this walk with the Lord, his life would have been much different. His pride and desire for power became his besetting sin. When the news got out that Saul had prophesied with a company of prophets, some of his friends spoke about him with disdain (1 Sam. 10:11-13).

There's no evidence that he was overly wicked, but Saul was a secular person, not a spiritual person, and he was the last man his friends ever expected to have that kind of experience. The question, "Is Saul also among the prophets?" was asked of anybody who suddenly stepped out of character and did the unexpected. Since prophets often inherited their ministry from their fathers (Amos 7:14), and were even called "fathers" (2 Kings 2:12; 6:2), the second question was asked: "Who is their father?" Even after Saul was presented to the people as their king, not everybody in Israel was impressed with him (1 Sam. 10:27).

Saul returned home and went back to work on the farm as though nothing remarkable had happened. He said nothing to his family about being anointed king, and apparently the news about his prophetic experiences hadn't reached as far as Gibeah. The experiences of the previous days should have taught him that God was with him (v. 7), and that He would take care of him and meet his needs, if only he would trust and obey. He also should have realized that he could trust Samuel to give him God's message, and that to disobey Samuel meant to disobey the Lord. One more task awaited Saul, and that was to meet Samuel at Gilgal at a time that would be shown him (v. 8). This would be a test to see if Saul was truly devoted to the Lord and willing to obey orders. Unfortunately, he failed.

Samuel presents Saul to the people (1 Sam. 10:17-27). Samuel called another convocation at Mizpah for the purpose of presenting the new king to the people. True to his prophetic calling, he first preached a sermon and reminded the people of their redemption from Egypt by God's grace and power as well as their obligation under the covenant to obey the Lord. But they had disobeyed the Lord in asking for a king! They had sinned, but the Lord would answer their request.

Only the Lord and Samuel knew that the king had already been selected and anointed, but Samuel wanted the tribes to realize that Jehovah was in charge of the selection process. He had the tribes present themselves, probably represented by their elders, and the tribe of Benjamin was selected. This may have been selection by lot (14:40-42), or one of the priests may have used the Urim and Thummim to determine the Lord's will (Ex. 28:30). The clan of Matri was selected next, and from that clan, the family of Kish and finally, the young man Saul.

But Saul couldn't be found! And Samuel had to inquire further of the Lord to discover that the king was hiding among the wagons and baggage, certainly not an auspicious way to begin his reign! Was he hiding out of modesty or fear? Probably the latter, because true humility accepts God's will while at the same time depending on God's strength and wisdom. As Andrew Murray said, "True humility isn't thinking meanly of one's self; it's simply not thinking of one's self at all." Had Saul been focusing on the glory of God, he would have been present in the assembly and humbly accepting God's call. Then he would have urged the people to pray for him and to follow him as he sought to do the Lord's will.

This first official act on the part of Saul suggests that there was trouble ahead. Saul was a reluctant ruler who followed his emotions instead of building his faith. He would serve as a sacrificing courageous soldier one day and become a self-centered autocrat the next day. Shunning national popularity is one thing, but shunning God-given responsibility is quite another. "If God called a man to kingship," said G. Campbell Morgan, "he has no right to hide away."[4] Samuel did what he could to salvage an embarrassing situation. He presented Saul as God's chosen king, so the nation had to accept him, and he accented Saul's admirable physical characteristics. The people were impressed, but Samuel certainly knew that God didn't need tall, muscular men in order to get His work done. In a few years, He would use teenage David to kill a giant! (See Ps. 147:10-11.)

The wisest thing Samuel did that day was to link the kingship with the divine covenant (1 Sam. 10:25). His first speech about the king had been negative (8:10-18), but this address and document were positive and pointed out the duties of both king and people. Samuel no doubt elaborated on Moses' words from Deuteronmy 17:14-20 and reminded the people that even the king had to submit to the Lord and His Word. There was one God, one nation, and one covenant, and the Lord was still in charge.

When the assembly was ended, everybody went back home, including the king, and there accompanied him a group of valiant men who became his officers and inner circle. They followed Saul because the Lord moved them to do so. People gave Saul gifts as tokens of their homage to the king, but one group of men despised and ridiculed him. As king, Saul could have dealt severely with them, but he held his peace. And yet later, he was willing to kill Jonathan his son just because the boy had eaten some honey! Saul's emotional instability had him weeping over David one day and trying to kill him the next.

4. Serving the Lord (1 Sam. 11:1-15)

One of the reasons Israel asked for a king was so the nation could unite behind one leader and have a better opportunity to face their enemies. The Lord condescended to reach down to their level of unbelief, and He gave them a king who looked like a natural warrior. How sad it is that God's people trusted a man of clay whom they could admire, and yet they would not trust the Lord who throughout the nation's history had proven Himself powerful on their behalf. In His grace, God gave Saul an opportunity to prove himself and consolidate his authority.

The challenge (1 Sam. 1-3). The Ammonites were descendants of Abraham's nephew Lot (Gen. 19:30-38) and therefore related to the Jewish people. The dangers posed by Nahash ("snake") and his army had helped to motivate the Jews to ask for a king, and now Nahash was encamped around Jabesh Gilead, a city about fifty miles from Saul's home. Rather than engage in a long and costly siege, Nahash offered to negotiate with the people in the city and let them live. All he demanded was that they submit to the humiliating and crippling punishment of having their right eyes gouged out. Archers and swordsmen would be handicapped in battle, and everybody would be humiliated and marked as defeated prisoners of war. Without having to kill anybody, Nahash could subdue the city, take its wealth, and enslave the people.

Wisely, the elders of the city asked for a week's delay, hoping to find somebody who could rescue them, and Nahash agreed, thinking that weak Israel couldn't muster an army. It's interesting that nobody from Jabesh Gilead responded to the call to arms when the nation had to punish the wickedness of Gilead in Benjamin (Jud. 21:8-9), but now they were asking their fellow Jews to come and rescue them!

The conquest (1 Sam. 11:4-11). It's strange that the messengers from Jabesh Gilead didn't hasten to contact Samuel and Saul first of all. Samuel their prophet had prayed and God gave victory over the Philistines, and Saul their new king had the nucleus of an army. It would take time for the Jews to get accustomed to the new form of government. When the news came, Saul was plowing in the field with the oxen. The Jews were noted for their loud and passionate expressions of grief, and when Saul heard the people weeping, he asked the cause. No sooner did the king understand the situation than he experienced an endowment of the Spirit of God and his own spirit was filled with righteous indignation that such a thing should happen in Israel.

Instantly Saul moved into action and in a dramatic way sent the message to the men of Israel that they were needed for battle. (Compare the actions of the Levite in Jud. 19.) He also identified himself with Samuel when he issued the call to arms, for he and Samuel were working together. The Lord worked on Saul's behalf by putting fear in the hearts of the people so that 330,000 men gathered for battle. Saul mustered the army at Bezek, about twenty miles from Jabesh Gilead, and then sent a message to the city that help was coming the next day before midmorning. Shrewdly, the citizens told the Ammonites that they would surrender the next day, and this gave Nahash the kind of false confidence that threw the army off-guard.

Saul may have known the story of Gideon and his defeat of the Midianites, because like Gideon he divided his army into three parts and attacked at night (Jud. 7:16, 19). The morning watch was from 2 to 6 A.M., so he caught the enemy by surprise and completely routed them. Saul succeeded because he was empowered by the Spirit of God who both used Saul's natural gifts and gave him the wisdom and strength he needed. Being at the head of an inexperienced army of 330,000 men wouldn't be an easy task, but God gave the victory. The will of God will never lead us where the grace of God can't keep us and use us.

When Saul was chosen king, he was given *authority* from God and from the nation, but when he won this great victory, he gained *stature* before the people. It takes both to be an effective leader. The difficulties began later when Saul's pride inflated his authority and began to destroy his character and his stature. David was humbled by his success, but Saul became more and more proud and abusive. We admire Saul for not using the victory as a means of getting rid of his enemies but for giving glory to the Lord (1 Sam. 11:13; Lev. 19:18; Rom. 12:17). Effective leaders use their authority to honor God and build up their people, but ineffective leaders use the people to build up their authority. Later on, Saul began to do that, and it led to his failure.

Samuel seized the opportunity and called the nation together to give thanks to the Lord and to affirm the king and the kingdom. They met at Gilgal, near the Jordan River, a place that had solemn associations for the Jews (Josh. 4:19-5:11; 7:16; 10:8-15; 13:4). At the Mizpah assembly, they had accepted God's king, but at Gilgal they confirmed Saul as king before the Lord (1 Sam. 12:1). Our modern word would be "coronation." The peace offerings were part of a covenant ceremony in which the people sacrificed to God and then had a meal of some of the portions of the animals they gave to God. It was clear to everybody that the king and the nation had entered into a renewed covenant relationship with the Lord and were responsible to obey Him.

Samuel had anointed Saul privately (10:1) and then presented him to the people (vv. 17-27), and now Samuel led the nation in an act of dedication to the Lord. It was a time of spiritual revival and national rejoicing. Saul had passed his first test, but it wouldn't be long before he would fail in a much simpler test and lose his kingdom. Saintly Andrew Bonar used to say, "We must be as watchful after the victory as before the battle." Saul won his first battle but he would lose the victory.

F O U R

Reviewing and Rebuking

Saul and the people rejoiced greatly over the deliverance of Jabesh Gilead from the Ammonites, and Saul was careful to give the glory to the Lord (11:13). Samuel saw the victory as a great opportunity to "renew the kingdom" (v. 14) and remind the people that Jehovah God was still their King. The fact that Saul had led the army in a great victory would tempt the Israelites to put their faith in their new king, and Samuel wanted them to know that their future success rested in trusting Jehovah alone. The king was only God's servant for the people, and both king and people had to obey God's covenant. In his farewell message, Samuel defended his own ministry (vv. 1-5), reviewed God's mercies to Israel (vv. 6-11), and admonished the people to fear the Lord and obey the covenant (vv. 12-25). Samuel mentions the Lord at least thirty times in this message, because his heart's desire was to see the people return to the Lord and honor His covenant.

1. A leader's integrity (1 Sam. 12:1-5)
In asking for a king, the people had rejected the kingship of Jehovah and the leadership of Samuel, the last of the judges (7:6,

59

15-17). It must have been painful for Samuel to conduct this last meeting as their leader and transfer the civil authority to Saul. No doubt he had hoped that one of his sons would succeed him, but they weren't even considered (8:1-3). The twelve tribes had been governed by judges for nearly 500 years, but times had changed and the people wanted a king. Before leaving office as judge, Samuel had to set the record straight and bear witness that his hands were clean and the people could find no fault in him.

To many of the people at that assembly, Samuel had "always been there." Some of them had known him when he was a child and youth at Shiloh, learning to serve as a priest, and others remembered when he had begun to proclaim the Word of the Lord (3:20). He had walked before them almost all of his life, and now he stood before them "old and gray-headed" and challenged them to accuse him of using his authority to benefit himself. "Here I am" (12:3) makes us think of Samuel's responses the night the Lord called him (3:4-6, 8, 16). In the East, it was expected that civil officials would use their offices to make money, but Samuel hadn't taken that route. He obeyed the Law of Moses and kept his hands clean (Ex. 20:17; 22:1-4, 9; 23:8; Lev. 19:13; Deut. 16:19; 24:14). With such a godly example before them, we wonder why his sons took bribes.

Like Jesus, Samuel stood before the people and asked, "Which of you convicts me of sin?" (John 8:46, NKJV). The people heard what Samuel said and bore witness that he had spoken the truth. Samuel was a man of integrity; Saul would turn out to be a man of hypocrisy and duplicity. When the assembly gave their vote of confidence to Samuel, the prophet called the Lord and the new king to bear witness to what they had said. If the people ever changed their mind, they would have to deal with God and His appointed king!

It's a wonderful thing to get to the closing years of life and be able to review your life and ministry and not be afraid or ashamed. May we all be able to say with our Lord, "I have glorified You on the earth. I have finished the work which You have given Me to do" (John 17:4, NKJV).

2. A nation's iniquity (1 Sam. 12:6-25)

Having affirmed Samuel's credibility, the people now had to accept his analysis of the situation. He reviewed Israel's history from Moses to his own day and emphasized what the Lord in His grace had done for them.

Thank the Lord (1 Sam. 6-11) It was God, not the people, who appointed Moses and Aaron (v. 6) and who enabled them to do the mighty works they did for the people of Israel. Samuel wasn't afraid to point out Israel's sins and then challenge them to devote themselves to the Lord and to His covenant. It's often been said that the one thing we learn from history is that we don't learn from history, and Samuel didn't want his people to make that mistake.

But this was more than a lecture on history; it was also a court trial. Samuel's words in verse 7 have a judicial flavor: "stand still" carries the idea of "Stand up, court is in session!" and "reason" means "to decide a case of litigation." Samuel was going to prove to the people that the Lord had been righteous and faithful in all His dealings with Israel, but that the Jews had been faithless and disobedient. The Lord had covenanted with no other nation on earth except Israel, and Israel's obedience to that covenant made possible their enjoyment of God's promised blessings. These blessings included living in the Promised Land, being protected from their enemies, and having fruitful fields, flocks and herds, and families. If they failed to obey, the Lord would discipline them and take away their blessings. (See Deut. 28–30 and Lev. 26.) Every Jew knew this, but not every Jew really understood it.

Israel in Egypt cried out to the Lord for help, and He sent them Moses and Aaron (1 Sam. 12:8). God delivered His people and took them to Canaan and gave them victory over the inhabitants of the land. But once they were in the land, they compromised their faith and joined in worshiping the false gods of their neighbors; so God had to discipline them (vv. 9-11). Now we are in the Book of Judges with its seven cycles of disobedience, discipline, and deliverance (Jud. 2:10-23). Samuel's point is that God always provided a leader when one was needed, and the nation wouldn't have needed a judge if the people had been faithful to God. In 1 Samuel 12:11, Jerubbaal ("let Baal contend [for himself]") is Gideon, and Bedan is probably Barak.[1] Samuel included himself, for he was the last of the judges (7:15).

Fear the Lord (1 Sam.12:12-19). How should Israel have responded to this kind of national history? They should have expressed gratitude to the Lord and trusted Him for His continued care. They should have confessed their sin of unbelief and trusted Him alone. But what did they do? No sooner did the Ammonites attack than the Jews asked for a king and exchanged the rule of the Lord their King for the leadership of a mere man! God gave them what they asked for, but Israel lost something in the transaction.

However, all was not lost. God is never taken by surprise and He would not desert His people for His name's sake. If the people would fear the Lord and follow Him, He would continue to care for them and use their king to direct and protect them. Then Samuel demonstrated the awesome power of the Lord by "praying up a storm" during the dry season of wheat harvest (mid-May to mid-June). This miracle reminds us of the signs Moses and Aaron did in Egypt. Samuel was proving to the people that God could do anything for them if they trusted Him and obeyed, but that a mere king was helpless apart from the Lord. When the Jews begged Samuel for deliverance, they sounded like Pharaoh confessing his sin and begging Moses for relief (Ex, 8:8; 9:27-28; 10:16-17), and their repentance was probably just as insincere.

Obey the Lord (1 Sam. 12:20-25). Samuel moved from "Fear" to "Fear not" as he encouraged the people to accept the situation their unbelief created and make the most of it. How many times in our own lives do we get what we asked for and then wish we didn't have it! The Lord would not reject or forsake His people because of His holy covenant and His great faithfulness. God's purpose was to use Israel to bring glory to His name, and He would fulfill that purpose. The Jewish people knew the terms of the covenant: if they obeyed, the Lord would bless them; if they disobeyed, He would chasten them. Either way, He would be faithful to His Word; the major issue was whether Israel would be faithful. They had made a mistake, but God would help them if they feared and obeyed Him.

Samuel made it clear that, no matter what they decided, he would obey the Lord. Part of his obedience would be faithfully praying for the people and teaching them the Word of God. The Word of God and prayer always go together (Acts 6:4; John 15:7; Eph. 6:17-18). Samuel's heart was broken, but as a faithful servant of the Lord, he interceded for the people and sought to lead them in the right way. For God's people not to pray is to sin against the Lord, yet if there's one thing lacking in our churches today, it is prayer, particularly prayer for those in authority (1 Tim. 2:1-4).

When we consider the great things God has done for us, how could we do other than fear Him, thank Him, and serve Him in truth all the days of our lives? God's covenant with His people Israel was still in force: if they obeyed, He would bless; if they disobeyed, He would chasten. "Yet if you persist in doing evil," warned Samuel, "both you and your king will be swept away" (1 Sam. 12:25). Samuel may have been referring especially to the warning given by Moses in Deut. 28:36, *written into the covenant centuries before Israel had a king*: "The Lord will drive you and the king you set over you to a nation unknown to you or your fathers" (NIV). Unfortunately, Israel did disobey the terms of the covenant and God had to send them in exile to Babylon.

From time to time, churches and other Christian ministries face new situations and decide they must make organizational changes. Each ministry needs a Samuel to remind them of the spiritual principles that never change: the character of God, the Word of God, the necessity of faith, and the importance of obedience.

> Methods are many, principles are few;
> Methods always change, principles never do.

As the old Youth for Christ slogan expressed it, "Geared to the times but anchored to the Rock." Some changes are inevitable and necessary, but they need not destroy the work of God.

3. A king's irresponsibility (1 Sam. 13:1-14)

The narrative in chapters 13–15 focuses on Saul's early reign, especially his relationship to God and to Samuel. We see Saul making foolish and unwise decisions and trying to cover his disobedience with lies. It was the beginning of that tragic decline that ended in a witch's house and Saul's suicide on the battlefield. At chapter 16, David will come on the scene and the book will describe Saul's deepening conflict with God, himself, and David. We can trace the downward steps in his tragic failure.

Pride (1 Sam. 13:1-4). Saul had reigned two years when he began to establish a standing army.[2] Over 300,000 men had volunteered to deliver the people of Jabesh Gilead (11:8), but Saul chose only 3,000 and divided them between himself and his son Jonathan. Saul's camp was at Michmash and Jonathan's was about fifteen miles away in Gibeah. The fact that Israel was mustering an army put the Philistines on the alert. They had garrisons in different parts of the country and monitored the situation carefully.

It is as a brave and victorious soldier that Jonathan is introduced to us. When he attacked and defeated the Philistine outpost at Geba, it was a declaration of war, and the Philistines were quick to respond. This was the beginning of Israel's war of liberation, although it wasn't finished until after David became king. But who blew the trumpet and seemed to take the credit for the victory? Saul, son of Kish! As commander-in-chief, he was calling for more men, because he knew that many battles lay ahead, but we wish he had given proper credit to his courageous son.

Why did Saul call his fellow Israelites "the Hebrews" instead of "men of Israel"? The name may have come from Abraham's ancestor Eber (Gen. 10:21), or perhaps from the word meaning "to cross over." The ancestors of Abraham were those who "crossed over the River Euphrates" (Josh. 24:2-3). Canaan was "the land of the Hebrews" (Gen. 40:15); the Egyptians would not eat with "the Hebrews" (43:32); an Egyptian "beat one of the Hebrews" (Ex. 2:11). In Scripture, the word is used primarily by foreigners speaking to or of the Jews, or by the Jews speaking to foreigners about themselves. You get the impression that the word "Hebrew" was often used as a term of contempt. Did Saul not have respect for his people? Whatever reason he had for using the word, his command was clear: gather together at Gilgal, the place that Samuel had appointed (1 Sam.10:8ff).

Unbelief and impatience (1 Sam. 13:5-9). The Philistine forces gathered at Michmash, less than twenty miles west of Gilgal, and it was obvious that Saul and his army were greatly outnumbered.[3] Saul's men began to hide and even deserted the army by crossing the river, and those who remained were paralyzed with fright. As Samuel had commanded, Saul waited for seven days (10:8), and the longer he waited, the more concerned he became. His army was melting away, the enemy was mobilizing, and the situation was hopeless.

Why did Samuel tarry? Was he deliberately trying to make Saul fail, or was he just reminding the new king who was still in control? Samuel had nothing to gain if Saul failed on the battlefield, and Samuel knew that God was in control, even in the appointment of the new king. Furthermore, this meeting had been planned some two years before (v. 8), and no doubt Samuel had reminded Saul of it more than once. *This rendezvous was the Lord's way of testing Saul's faith and patience.* Without faith and patience, we can't receive what the Lord promises (Heb. 6:12), and unbelief and impatience are marks of spiritual immaturity (James 1:1-8). Until we learn to trust God and wait on His timing, we can't learn the other lessons He wants to teach us, nor can we receive the blessings He's planned for us. Saul may have been handsome, strong, and taller than the other men, but if he didn't have a heart that was right with God, he didn't have anything. It's one thing to be victorious when you're leading an army of over 300,000 men (1 Sam. 11:8), but quite another thing when you have only 600! (v. 15) But this is where faith comes in.

Saul didn't want to go into the battle without first offering a sacrifice to the Lord, which in itself may have been a subtle form of superstition, like carrying the ark into the battle. Later Samuel would remind Saul that God seeks obedience and not sacrifice

(15:22). Without waiting for God's appointed priest, Saul offered the sacrifice, and just then Samuel arrived in the camp. If Saul had waited just a few minutes more, everything would have been all right; but his impatience cost him dearly.

Deception (1 Sam. 13:10-12). As Saul decays in character, we shall see him deceiving himself and others more and more. His first deception at Gilgal occurred when he greeted Samuel cordially and expected Samuel to give him a blessing. Saul was playing the hypocrite and acting as though he had done nothing wrong. "If we say that we have fellowship with him, and walk in darkness, we lie, and do not the truth" (1 John 1:6, KJV). His second lie consisted in blaming Samuel and the soldiers and not himself. It was Samuel's fault for arriving late and the army's fault for deserting their king. His words, "I saw" indicate that Saul was walking by sight and not by faith. He lied a third time when he said that he had to force himself to offer the sacrifice. Could he not have "forced himself" to pray or to call together some of the officers to beseech the Lord for His help? The will is the servant of the mind and heart, but Saul's thinking and desiring were totally out of the will of God.

People who are good at making excuses are rarely good at anything else, and those who are quick to blame others shouldn't complain if others blame them. When God confronted our first parents with their sin, Adam blamed Eve, and Eve blamed the serpent, but neither Adam nor Eve said humbly, "I have sinned." Throughout his career, King Saul was adept at minimizing his own sins and emphasizing the faults of others, but this isn't the way a man of God leads God's people.

Folly (1 Sam. 13:13-14).[4] It was foolish of Saul to think that he could disobey God and get away with it, and that his disobedience could bring God's blessing on himself and his army. "Let us do evil that good may come" (Rom. 3:8) is the logic of hell, not the law of heaven. He was foolish to conclude that the sacrifice of a king at the wrong time was as good as the sacrifice of a priest at the right time. He was foolish to walk by sight and not by faith in God's promise, "for whatsoever is not of faith is sin"

(Rom. 14:23, KJV). Saul had the same kind of superstitious faith that Eli's sons had when they carried the ark on the battlefield. He knew nothing of "the obedience of faith" (Rom. 16:26).

Saul's pride, impatience, disobedience, and deception were all seen and judged by the Lord, and Samuel announced the sentence: the crown would eventually be taken from Saul and given to another, in this case, David. Saul would continue as king, but he would not establish a lasting dynasty, and none of his sons would succeed him and rule over Israel. But even if Saul had not sinned, how could his dynasty continue "forever" (1 Sam. 13:13) when Saul was from the wrong tribe and God had already chosen David to be king of Israel? One answer is that Saul's eldest son Jonathan could have served with David, which in fact is what David and Jonathan had planned (20:31, 42; 23:16-18). Of course, the Davidic dynasty would have established the Messianic line, but someone from Saul's family would have served in court with the Davidic king.

Saul's sin at Gilgal cost him the dynasty, and his sin involving the Amalekites cost him the kingdom. He eventually lost his crown and his life (see 15:16-34, especially 23, 27-29; 16:1). God wanted a king with a heart that was right toward God, a man with a shepherd's heart, and He found that kind of heart in David (13:14; Pss. 78:72; 89:20; Acts 13:22). "This man [Saul] in his governing of Israel was a warrior and nothing more," said G. Campbell Morgan; "he was never a shepherd." But David had a shepherd's heart, because the Lord was his Shepherd (Ps. 23:1). David was under authority, so he had the right to exercise authority.

4. An army's insecurity (1 Sam. 13:15-23)

Saul had failed miserably, but in chapter 14 we will read about Jonathan's great success as a commander. This passage describes the sad condition of the army of Israel, which reveals how poor Saul's leadership was and how remarkable Jonathan's victory was. Saul walked by sight and had little faith, but Jonathan walked by faith and did exploits for the Lord.

A *dwindling army* (1 Sam. 13:15-16). Saul had mustered over

300,000 men to rescue the people of Jabesh Gilead and then had cut it down to 3,000, but now his forces numbered only 600. The Philistine army was "as the sand which is on the seashore in multitude" (v. 5), a simile also used for the army Gideon faced (Jud. 7:12)—and Saul's army was twice as large as Gideon's! The difference wasn't so much the size of the army as the strength of the leader's faith. Gideon trusted God for victory and God honored him; Saul disobeyed God and God punished him. Saul had mustered that huge army by means of fear (1 Sam. 11:7), so when his men began to fear the enemy instead of the king, they began to desert the camp and go to places of safety. Jonathan knew that the Lord didn't need great numbers to accomplish His purposes (14:6), but He did honor great faith.

A *threatened army* (1 Sam. 13:17-18, 23). The Philistines repeatedly sent out "raiding parties" to protect the roads and passes that the Jews might use if they attacked, and at the same time the Philistines kept any residents from helping the Jewish army. There were three such groups: one went north toward Ophrah, a second west to Beth-horon, and the third east toward Zeboim. A fourth detachment went south toward Gibeah to prevent the Jewish army from moving up to Geba (v. 23). With all these Philistine soldiers moving about in the area, what hope was there for the Jews? No matter which way Israel turned, they would meet the enemy! And yet the Lord was going to use Jonathan and his armor-bearer to win a great victory, for with God, nothing is impossible.

A *deprived army* (1 Sam. 13:19-22). It was bad enough that Saul lacked men, but it was even worse that his men were not properly equipped. When the Philistines moved in and subjected the land of Israel to their rule, they deported all the ironworkers so that the Jews couldn't make weapons or even repair their farm implements. They even had to pay exorbitant prices to have their implements sharpened. The Benjamites were skilled at using slings (Jud. 20:15-16), but slings were not practical in close combat, and what about the vast number of Philistine chariots? The Jewish army was small in number and had small supplies of weapons, but they had a great God, if only they would trust Him. All of this sets the stage for Jonathan's thrilling victory described in chapter 14, and that is contrasted with his father's sad defeat in chapter 15.

In the way it functions or doesn't function, the church of Jesus Christ today may sometimes resemble Saul's army, but if we do, it's our own fault. Through His great work on the cross, our Lord has defeated every enemy, and His power is available to His people. We have the armor and the weapons we need (Eph. 6:10ff), and His Word tells us all we need to know about the strategy of the enemy and the resources we have in Christ. All He asks is that we trust Him and obey His orders, and He will help us win the battle.

"Be strong in the Lord, and in the power of his might" (Eph. 6:10, KJV) for "the battle is the Lord's" (1 Sam. 17:47).

FIVE

A Foolish Vow and a Lame Excuse

Our task isn't an enjoyable one as we watch the character of King Saul steadily deteriorate. He has already demonstrated his unbelief and impatience (chap. 13), and now he will reveal further his disobedience and dishonesty. Saul's history will climax with the king visiting a witch and then committing suicide on the battlefield. Sir Walter Scott was right when he wrote in his poem "Marmion"

> O what a tangled web we weave
> When first we practice to deceive!

These chapters teach us three powerful lessons that we must heed and obey if we want the blessing of God on our lives and service.

1. Faith in God brings victory (1 Sam. 14:1-23)

The focus in this chapter is on Jonathan, Saul's oldest son, who had won the first major battle against the Philistines, but his father had taken the credit (13:1-7). It's a remarkable blessing of the grace of God that a man like Saul should have a son so magnificent as Jonathan. He was a courageous warrior (2 Sam. 1:22), a born leader, and a man of faith who sought to do the will of God. As the account progresses, it becomes clear that Saul is jealous of Jonathan and his popularity, and this jealousy increases when Jonathan and David became devoted friends.

Jonathan initiates the attack (1 Sam. 14:1-15). The Philistines had sent a detachment of soldiers to establish a new outpost to guard the pass at Michmash (13:23), and Jonathan saw this as an opportunity to attack and see the Lord work. Saul was hesitating in unbelief (14:2) while his son was acting by faith. God had called Saul to begin Israel's liberation from the Philistines, but most of the time he only followed up on what others started. In spite of all that the Lord had done for him and all that Samuel had taught him, Saul was not a man of faith who trusted the Lord and sought to glorify Him. Saul had a priest of the Lord attending him, a man named Ahijah from the rejected line of Eli (v. 3), but the king never waited for the Lord's counsel (vv. 18-20). Saul is a tragic example of the popular man of the world who tries to appear religious and do God's work, but who lacks a living faith in God and a heart to honor Him. Unfortunately, church history records the lives of too many gifted people who "used God" to achieve their own purposes, but in the end abandoned Him and ended life in disgrace.

Why didn't Jonathan tell his father that he had a plan to rout the enemy? Because Saul in unbelief would have vetoed such a daring venture of faith, and Jonathan had no desire to disagree with him at such a crucial time. Jonathan may have been insubordinate to his father and commander-in-chief, but his plan was still the wisest approach to take. With their false sense of security, the Philistine troops at the new outpost wouldn't be afraid of a couple of Jews who managed to cross the pass and climb the cliffs. Maybe the guards would see them as two Jewish men who wanted to desert the Hebrew army and find refuge with the enemy. Jonathan wasn't about to let the enemy attack first.

You can't help but admire Jonathan's faith in the Lord. Perhaps as he climbed the rocks, he meditated on God's promises of victory stated in the covenant. "You will chase your enemies, and they shall fall by the sword before you. Five of you shall chase a hundred, and a hundred of you shall put ten thousand to flight; your enemies shall fall by the sword before you" (Lev. 26:7-8, NKJV; see Deut. 28:7). Action without promises is presumption, not faith, but when you have God's promises, you can go forward with confidence. Jonathan may also have been thinking of Gideon when he told his armor-bearer, "Perhaps the Lord will help us, for nothing can hinder the Lord. He can win a battle whether he has many warriors or only a few" (1 Sam. 14:6, NLT; see Jud. 6-7). "If God be for us, who can be against us?" (Rom. 8:31)

But Jonathan's plan of attack differed from Gideon's in at least two ways: It was not a surprise attack at night, and he and his armor-bearer deliberately let themselves be seen by the Philistine guards. It was the guards' response that would give Jonathan the guidance he needed.[1] Should Jonathan wait for the Philistines to come over or should he go over and meet them on their own ground? When the two men disclosed themselves to the enemy, the Philistines only laughed and mocked them. They treated them like frightened animals that had emerged from their burrows or like soldiers who were deserting the Hebrew cause and joining the Philistine army.

This kind of arrogant self-confidence was exactly what Jonathan wanted to see, because this gave him and his armor-bearer opportunity to get close to the guards before attacking. Who would fear one soldier and his armor-bearer? But these two men had Almighty God on their side! "One of you routs a thousand, because the Lord your God fights for you, just as he promised" (Josh. 23:10). The two courageous Jews quickly killed twenty men, and then the Lord honored their faith by sending an earthquake, "a very great trembling"! "But the Lord your God will deliver them over to you, throwing them into great confusion until they are destroyed" (Deut. 7:23). Terror and confusion gripped the enemy camp and prepared the way for a great victory of the army of Israel.

Saul watches the battle (1 Sam. 14:16-19). Saul and his 600 men were back at Gibeah where Saul lived, and the watchmen on the walls could see the Philistine forces retreating and couldn't explain why. Did part of the Israeli army plan a sneak attack without Saul's permission? Who was missing? Jonathan and his armor-bearer! This was the second time that Jonathan had acted on his own (13:3), and it probably irritated Saul that his own son should be so independent. As we study the life of Saul, we will see more and more evidence that he was what some people call a "control freak." He envied other people's success, he was suspicious of any strategy he didn't originate or at least approve, and he was ruthless when it came to removing people who challenged his leadership or exposed his folly.

Saul asked the priest to bring him the ark of the Lord and probably also the ephod.[2] He was probably planning to take the ark to the battlefield with the army, a foolish tactic that had brought judgment in Eli's day (chap. 4); and the priest could use the ephod to determine God's will in the matter. But the priest never had a chance to determine God's will, for when Saul heard the noise of the battle increasing, he interrupted the divine proceedings and made his own decision. Once again, Saul's impatience and self-confidence got the best of him and he acted without knowing God's will or receiving God's blessing (Deut. 20:4-5). He was desperately anxious to prove himself as good a soldier as Jonathan and he desperately wanted to avenge himself against his enemies (1 Sam. 14:24). It was to fulfill his own personal agenda, not to honor God, that he rushed into the battle spiritually unprepared.

Israel enters the battle (1 Sam. 14:20-23). As Saul and his army moved toward the battlefield, they were joined by Israelites who had deserted to the enemy camp (v. 21) and by men who had fled the battle and hidden away (v. 22). We wonder what kind of soldiers these quitters turned out to be. The fact that Saul accepted these men may indicate that he was trusting his army and not trusting the Lord. Six hundred soldiers don't make a large army, so he welcomed even the weakest man to return. Yet in a few hours, Saul would be willing to kill his own son for eating some honey and breaking his father's foolish vow! Saul's emotional unbalance and contradictory thinking will show up again and again and do great damage to the kingdom. One day he will rush ahead like the horse, and the next day he will hold back like the mule (Ps. 32:9).

It was not Saul and his army who won the battle, but the Lord who used Jonathan and his armor-bearer (1 Sam. 14:23, see vv. 6, 12, and 45). The Israelite army followed the Philistines for the next fifteen miles, from Michmash to Beth Aven, and the Lord enabled them to defeat the enemy. But Saul had joined the battle so late, and his men were so weak and famished, that he couldn't achieve the kind of victory that would have been decisive (v. 30). One of the marks of a true leader is knowing when to act, and Saul had wasted time watching the battle from a distance and failing to seek the mind of the Lord.

2. Foolish words bring trouble (1 Sam. 14:24-52)

The spiritual conditions of our hearts are revealed not only by the actions we perform but also by the words we speak. "For out of the abundance of the heart the mouth speaks" (Matt. 12:34). When you read King Saul's words recorded in Scripture, they often reveal a heart controlled by pride, foolishness, and deceit. He would say foolish things just to impress people with his "spirituality," when in reality he was walking far from the Lord.

A foolish vow (1 Sam. 14:24-35). Saul's heart was not right with God and he foolishly forced his army to agree to a vow of fasting until evening (v. 24). He didn't impose this fast because it was the will of God but because he wanted his soldiers to think he was a man wholly dedicated to the Lord. But this command was only more evidence of Saul's confused and superstitious faith. He thought that their fasting plus the presence of the ark would impress the Lord and He would give them victory. But Jonathan and his armor-bearer were already enjoying victory without either the ark or the fast!

No sensible commander would deprive his troops of food and energy while they were fighting the enemy. If the Lord commands it, then He would give the strength needed, but God gave Saul no such commission. Moses had fasted for forty days and nights when he was on the mountain with the Lord (Ex. 34:28), for the Lord sustained him. But Saul's soldiers were "distressed" (1 Sam. 14:24), "faint" (v. 28), and "very faint" (v. 31) because of this unnecessary fast. When we obey God's commands, we walk by faith, but when we obey unnatural human regulations, we only tempt the Lord. The first is confidence but the second is presumption. All of us need to heed the admonition given in Eccl. 5:2—"Do not be rash with your mouth, and let not your heart utter anything hastily before God" (NKJV).

When Jonathan and his armor-bearer joined the Israelite army in their march, they knew nothing about the king's foolish command, and Jonathan ate some honey from a honeycomb that had dropped to the ground. Then one of the soldiers told him that his father had put a curse on any soldier who ate any food that day. Why hadn't somebody warned Jonathan sooner? Perhaps they hoped that his innocent "disobedience" would open the way for all of them to eat! We wonder if Saul wasn't deliberately putting his son's life in jeopardy. However, Jonathan wasn't too worried, and he even dared to admit that his father's leadership had brought trouble to the land (v. 29).

Saul's foolish vow not only weakened the soldiers physically and hindered their ability to pursue the enemy, but it also created in the men an abnormal craving for food. When the sun set and ushered in a new day, the vow was no longer in force, and the men acted like animals as they fell on the spoils, killing the sheep and oxen and eating the meat with the blood. When Jews slaughtered their animals, they were required to drain out the blood before preparing the meat, for blood was never to be used as food (Lev. 3:17; 7:26; 17:10-14; 22:28; Deut. 12:23-24; see Gen. 9:4). A truly spiritual vow brings out the best in people, but Saul's carnal vow brought out the worst.

As he often did, the king assumed "spiritual leadership" and commanded the men to bring the animals to a great rock to be slain and the blood easily drained out. He then built an altar so that the animals could be offered as fellowship offerings (Lev. 3; 7:11-34), parts of which the people were allowed to eat in a fellowship feast. Saul was feebly trying to turn a gastronomical orgy into a worship service, but he didn't succeed too well. The men were famished and more interested in eating than in worshiping the Lord.

A foolish judgment (1 Sam. 14:36-52). Surely Saul realized that his delay at Gibeah and the imposing of the foolish vow had already cost the Israelites a great victory, so he tried to make amends. He decided to move the army that very night and be ready to surprise the Philistines early the next morning. The army gave no resistance, but Ahijah the priest wisely suggested that they pause long enough to seek the will of the Lord. We aren't told what method Ahijah used to ascertain God's will, but whatever it was, God didn't answer. Even though Saul was not a godly man, his oath made in the Lord's name was legitimate; and if the Lord had ignored it, He would have dishonored His own name. Furthermore, the Lord was using this event to rebuke Saul as well as to honor Jonathan. Saul would discover that his men loved Jonathan and were prepared to defend him.

Saul already knew that Jonathan had been missing from the ranks (v. 17) and therefore he assumed that his son knew nothing about the vow. But if he had learned about the vow and still violated it, that made him an even greater sinner. Either way, Jonathan would be guilty and could be slain. We get the impression that Saul was almost determined that he would demote or destroy his own son, and it's clear that Jonathan didn't agree with his father's policies and practices. Hence, Saul made another oath (v. 39), and because his heart wasn't right nor his motive holy, he was taking the Lord's name in vain (Ex. 20:7).

This time they cast lots and the lot pointed to Saul and Jonathan. The second lot fell upon Jonathan. God could have changed the results (Prov. 16:33), but He wanted to bring the whole thing out in the open and humiliate King Saul, whose pride had caused the problem to begin with. The people praised Jonathan, not Saul, as the man who had brought the great victory to Israel, and if the Lord had used Jonathan in such a wonderful way, why should he be executed? By the time this matter was settled, it was too late to follow the Philistine army, so Saul and his men retreated. The victory did send the Philistines back home for a time, but they repeatedly threatened Israel (1 Sam. 14: 52). This victory did enhance Saul's reputation and helped him consolidate his kingdom. In verses 47-48 and 52, the writer summarizes some of Saul's major victories and informs us that he drafted every good man he met.

The facts about the royal family are summarized in vv. 49-51, but when they are compared with other texts (1 Sam. 9:2; 2 Sam. 21:8;1 Chron. 8:29-33; 9:39), they reveal some problems. Saul's grandfather was Abiel and his father Kish (1 Sam. 9:1-2). Ner was his uncle and Abner ("son of Ner") was captain of the army (14:51). Only three sons are mentioned (Jonathan, Ishvi, and Malchishua), while later texts speak also of Abinadab and Esh-Baal (1 Chron. 8:33; 9:39). He had two daughters, Merab and Michel, and all of these children were by his wife Ahinoam. His concubine Rizpah bore him Armoni and Mephibosheth (2 Sam. 21:8).

Jonathan, Malchishua and Abinadab all died with their father at Gilboa (1 Sam. 31:1-2), and Abner made Ish-bosheth king (2 Sam. 2:8ff). Ish-bosheth is probably the Esh-Baal of 1 Chronicles 8:33 and 9:39, for it wasn't unusual for Jewish men to have more than one name. But what happened to Ishvi? Was this also another name for Esh-Baal (Ish-bosheth), for the two names are not found together in any text. If so, then Saul had four sons by Ahinoam—Jonathan, the eldest, and then Ishhvi/Esh-Baal/Ish-bosheth, Malachishua, and Abinadab. Since the eldest and two youngest sons were killed in battle, this left Ish-Bosheth/Ishvi/Esh-Baal, Saul's second-born, to claim the crown. Of course, it's possible that Ishvi had died earlier, and this would have left Esh-Baal/Ish-bosheth to reign, or if Esh-Baal died, then Ishvi/Ish-bosheth survived to rule briefly.

3. Disobedience and deception bring judgment (1 Sam. 15:1-35)

This is a pivotal chapter in the story of Saul. The Lord gave him another opportunity to prove himself, but he failed again, lied about it, and was judged. Saul had a habit of substituting saying for doing and of making excuses instead of confessing his sins. No matter what happened, it was always somebody else's fault. He was more concerned about looking good before the people than being good before God. Consider the stages in this event that cost Saul the kingdom and eventually his life.

Disobeying God (1 Sam. 15:1-11). The Amalekites descended from Esau, the unbelieving brother of Jacob (Gen. 36:12, 15-16; Heb. 12:14-17) and the enemy of the Jewish people. The army of Amalek attacked the Jews shortly after Israel left Egypt, and they were defeated because God heard Moses' prayers and helped Joshua's army. At that time, the Lord declared perpetual war against Amalek (Ex. 17:8-16) and Balaam prophesied Amalek's ultimate defeat (Num. 24:20). See also Deuteronmy 25:17-19.

Some people find it difficult to believe that the Lord would command an entire nation to be destroyed just because of what their ancestors had done centuries before. Some of these critics may depend more on sentiment than on spiritual truth, not realizing how long-suffering the Lord had been with these nations and how unspeakably wicked they were (see 1 Sam. 15:18, 33; Gen. 15:16). God's covenant with the Jewish nation includes the promise, "I will curse him who curses you" (12:3), and God always keeps His Word. Nations like the Amalekites who wanted to exterminate the Jews weren't just waging war on Israel; they were opposing Almighty God and His great plan of redemption for the whole world. People are either for the Lord or against Him, and if they are against Him, they must suffer the consequences. Knowing God's covenant with Abraham, Saul allowed the Kenites to escape (1 Sam. 15:6) because they had befriended Israel. They were descendants of the Midianites, and Moses married a Midianite woman (Ex. 2:16, 21-22; see Jud. 4:11). History shows that nations that have persecuted Israel have been severely judged.

We admire Saul for being careful to protect the Kenites, but he wasn't careful to obey God's will. Everything that was vile and worthless he destroyed, but he permitted King Agag to live, and he allowed the Israelite soldiers to save "the best" of the flocks and herds. But if the Lord says something is condemned, how can we say it's "the best"? "Woe to those who call evil good and good evil" (Isa. 5:20, NKJV). Saul certainly had sufficient men to get the job done right, but he decided to do it his own way. The prophet Samuel knew about Saul's disobedience before the army returned from the battle and it grieved him. The Hebrew word means "to burn" and suggests a righteous indignation, a holy anger. For the remainder of his life, Samuel mourned over Saul (1 Sam. 16:1) and cried out to God (15:11).

Serving God acceptably involves doing the will of God in the right way, at the right time, and for the right motive. God had given Saul another chance and he had failed miserably. No wonder his mentor Samuel was angry and brokenhearted. Saul was God's choice for king and Samuel wanted him to succeed. In the end, Saul's failure to exterminate all the Amalekites resulted in his own death (2 Sam. 1:1-10).

In the matter of God's "repenting" (1 Sam. 15:11), there is no contradiction between this statement and verse 29. (See endnote 4.)

Saul lies to Samuel (1 Sam. 15:12-15). In the eyes of the soldiers and the Jewish people, Saul had won a great victory over a long-time enemy, but in God's eyes he was a failure. Yet the king was so impressed with himself that he went to Carmel and erected a stone monument in his honor and then went to Gilgal, where he had previously failed the Lord and Samuel (13:4ff). Was he trying to avoid meeting Samuel? Perhaps, but his efforts were futile. It was fifteen miles from Samuel's home in Ramah to Gilgal, perhaps a day's journey for the old prophet.

Saul's greeting was sheer hypocrisy. He had no blessing to give Samuel and he had not performed the will of the Lord. First he lied to himself in thinking he could get away with the deception, and then he lied to Samuel who already knew the truth. He even tried to lie to God by saying he would use the spared animals for sacrifices! (See 1 John 1:5-10.) Saul blamed the soldiers for sparing the spoils, but surely as their commander-in-chief, he could have controlled them. "They" spared the best, but "we" utterly destroyed the rest! With Saul, it was always somebody else's fault.

Saul argues with Samuel (1 Sam. 15:16-23). Does Samuel's emphatic "Stop!" suggest that Saul was turning away, or does it mean "Stop telling lies"? Perhaps both are true, for Saul had no great desire to discuss his affairs with Samuel. But Samuel had a message from the Lord, and Saul knew he had better listen. The day would come when Saul would give anything to hear a word from the Lord (28:4-6).

Saul had once been a modest young man (9:21), but now for the second time he had willfully disobeyed the Lord's will and even erected a monument in honor of the event. He was to annihilate a nation that for centuries had done evil, but he ended up doing evil himself. Confronted with this accusation, Saul began to argue with God's servant and deny that he had done wrong. For the second time he lied when he said, "I have obeyed" (15:13, 20); for the second time he blamed his army (vv. 15, 21); and for the second time he used the feeble excuse of dedicating the spared animals as sacrifices for the Lord (vv. 15, 21).

The prophet rejected all three lies and explained why God couldn't accept the animals as legitimate sacrifices: the Lord wants living obedience from the heart, not dead animals on the altar. God doesn't need any donations from us (Ps. 50:7-15), and the sacrifice He desires is a broken and contrite heart (51:16-17). Sacrifice without obedience is only hypocrisy and empty religious ritual (Isa. 1:11-17; Jer. 7:21-26; Ps. 40:6-8). "For I desire mercy, and not sacrifice, and the knowledge of God more than burnt offerings" (Hosea 6:6, KJV). The religious leaders in Jesus' day didn't understand this truth (Matt. 9:9-13; 12:1-8), although occasionally somebody in the crowd would see the light (Mark 12:28-34).

Samuel was a Levite and a prophet, so he certainly wasn't criticizing the Jewish sacrificial system. The Lord through Moses had established Jewish worship and it was right for the people to bring their sacrifices to the Lord. This was His appointed way of worship. But the worshipers had to come to the Lord with submissive hearts and genuine faith, or their sacrifices were in vain.

When David was in the wilderness and away from the priests and the sanctuary of God, he knew that God would accept worship from his heart. "Let my prayer be set before you as incense, the lifting up of my hands as the evening sacrifice" (Ps. 141:2, NKJV). Christian worship today must be more than simply going through a liturgy; we must worship God "in spirit and in truth" (John 4:24), "singing with grace in your hearts to the Lord" (Col. 3:16, NKJV).

But the prophet went on to reveal that the sins of rebellion and stubbornness (arrogance) controlled Saul's heart, and in God's sight, they were as evil as witchcraft and idolatry. (Later, Saul would actually resort to witchcraft.) Both sins were evidences of a heart that had rejected the Word of the Lord. To know God's will and deliberately disobey it is to put ourselves above God and therefore become our own god. This is the vilest form of idolatry.

Saul is rejected by God (1 Sam. 15:24-29). King Saul now moves from "I have obeyed the voice of the Lord" (v. 20) to "I have sinned."[3] However, this was not a true expression of repentance and sorrow for sin, because when he repeated it later, he added, "Honor me now...before the elders of my people" (v. 30). He was obviously more concerned about his reputation with the people than his character before God, and that is not the attitude of a man truly broken because of sin. Saul also admitted that he spared Agag and the animals because he feared the people instead of fearing the Lord and His commandment. But this was just another indication that he was more interested in being popular with people than in pleasing God.

Samuel refused to join Saul at the altar because he knew the Lord wouldn't receive the king's worship because He had rejected him. In his previous disobedience, Saul forfeited the dynasty (13:14), but now he lost his throne. He was no longer the king of Israel because Samuel would anoint young David to be king. Saul had already been warned about this judgment and now it would be fulfilled. As Samuel turned away, Saul clutched at the tassels on the hem of his garment (Num. 15:38-39) and tore the prophet's robe (see 1 Kings 11:29-39.) Samuel used the occurrence as an object lesson and announced that God had torn the kingdom from Saul's hand. Samuel called the Lord "the Strength of Israel," a name that speaks of God's glory, eminence, and perfection. How could such a wonderful God be guilty of changing or of telling lies? The Lord had announced that Saul would lose the kingdom, and nothing could change His mind.[4]

Saul is rejected by Samuel (1 Sam. 15:30-35). The Word of God simply did not penetrate Saul's mind and heart, and he continued to worry about maintaining his reputation rather than getting right with the Lord. Why Samuel changed his mind and decided to worship with Saul is a bit of a mystery, but the prophet's actions after that left no doubt where Samuel stood with reference to the king. Samuel publicly butchered King Agag and in that way let it be known that the king had failed to fulfill his commission. Samuel returned to his home in Ramah and Saul to his home in Gibeah, and Samuel made no more trips to see the king, either publicly or privately. Saul did visit Samuel once in Ramah (19:23-24).

Our hearts go out to Samuel who certainly suffered much because of the people and the king they so desperately wanted. When the kingdom was introduced in Israel, Samuel was replaced by a leader who was inferior to him in every way. Samuel did his best to advise the king and strengthen the kingdom, but Saul insisted on having his own way. Each time Saul was assigned a task, he failed, and when he was confronted, he lied and blamed others. When Israel experienced victories, it was usually Jonathan who led the way. It was a difficult time for Samuel, but God was still on the throne and had His true king waiting to be anointed.

King Saul had lost his dynasty, his character, and his throne and crown. He had also lost a godly friend. When David appears on the scene, Saul will lose his self-control and his good sense, and eventually he will lose his last battle—and his life.

SIX

God Chooses a King

Anyone who has ever been deeply disappointed by a friend or family member can understand why aged Samuel mourned so long over King Saul. Israel had rejected Samuel's leadership over them because he was too old, and they didn't want his sons to succeed him because they accepted bribes and perverted justice (8:3). But King Saul was guilty of disobeying God's clear commandments and also lying about what he had done, and because of these sins, he had forfeited his throne. He was still in office and yet was unfit to lead the nation, and Samuel had broken fellowship with him (15:34-35). In his grief, Samuel must have felt like a dismal failure as a father, a spiritual leader, and a mentor to the new king. The word translated "mourn" means "to mourn for the dead" and reveals the depths of Samuel's sorrow.

There is a time to mourn (Ecc. 3:4), but there is also a time to act (Josh. 7:10), and for Samuel, that time had arrived. In spite of how he felt about himself, Samuel's work wasn't over yet, for God wanted him to anoint the new king, David, the son of Jesse. If Saul was "the people's king," then David was God's king, and the events recorded in these two chapters indicate clearly that God's hand was unquestionably on David, the leader of His choice.

1. God chose David (16:1-13)

Had an election been held in Israel to choose a replacement for King Saul, it's not likely that the people would have chosen David, but he was God's first choice. "He also chose David his servant, and took him from the sheepfolds; from following the ewes that had young he brought him, to shepherd Jacob his people, and Israel his inheritance" (Ps. 78:70-71, NKJV). Let's consider some facts about this unusual young man.

David's city—Bethlehem (1 Sam. 16:1-5). In spite of the fact that it was a small town in Judah, Bethlehem was a well-known place to the Jewish people. It was when Jacob and his family were on their way to Bethel that his favorite wife, Rachel, died near Bethlehem while giving birth to Benjamin (Gen. 35:16-20). It was in Bethlehem that Ruth, the widow from Moab, found her husband, Boaz, and gave birth to Obed, David's grandfather (Ruth 4:13-22; Matt. 1:3-6). David himself would make Bethlehem a famous place, and so would Jesus, the Son of David, who would be born there as the Scriptures promised (Micah 5:2; Matt. 2:6). Bethlehem means "house of bread," and it was there that the living bread from heaven came to dwell in human flesh.

As Israel's judge and prophet, Samuel had the right to travel where he pleased in serving the Lord and His people. But these were difficult and dangerous times because Saul was a suspicious man and his spies would report anything Samuel did. From Samuel's home in Ramah, the road to Bethlehem passed by Gibeah where Saul had his headquarters, and Saul would want to know where Samuel was going and why he was going there. To avoid problems, God commanded His servant to take a heifer and announce that he would sacrifice a fellowship offering in Bethlehem for a select group of people, including Jesse and his sons. Then God would show Samuel which one to anoint as king.

The elders in Bethlehem knew that Saul and Samuel were estranged, so the arrival of Samuel gave them great alarm. Was Samuel recruiting followers to resist Saul? Would Saul interpret his presence in their little town as a declaration of war? Samuel quickly allayed their fears and told them to sanctify themselves and come to the sacrifice and the feast that would follow. "Sanctifying" meant that each of the guests would take a bath and change clothes (Ex. 19:10-15), because nobody ceremonially unclean could partake of the sacrificial feast (Lev. 7:19-21). For Jesse and his sons to be invited to this feast was a high honor, and, of course, nobody but Samuel knew why they were included.

David's family (1 Sam. 16:6-10). Before the guests sat down to enjoy the fellowship feast, Samuel looked over seven of Jesse's sons, thinking that the whole family was there, but he was operating by sight and not by faith. We don't know what Samuel's two sons looked like, but we do know that their father admired men who were handsome and well-built. Samuel had already forgotten this mistake he made about Saul (9:2; 10:23-24). David was the eighth son and only six of his brothers are named in Scripture: Eliab, the firstborn; Abinadab, the second; Shimea, the third, also called Shammah; Nethanel, or Nathaniel, the fourth; Raddai, the fifth; and Ozem, the sixth (1 Chron. 2:13-15). David is called the seventh in this genealogy, but 1 Samuel 16:10-11 makes it clear that he was the eighth and youngest son. Apparently one brother died without issue and his name dropped out of the genealogy. David also had two sisters: Zeruiah was the mother of Abishai, Joab, and Asahel; and Abigail, who was the mother of Amasa (1 Chron. 2:16-17). All of these men played important roles in David's kingdom.

No doubt there was no family in Bethlehem that could boast having seven such brothers, men of strength and stature, *and yet none of them was God's chosen king!* Samuel may have looked at their faces and forms, but the Lord examined their hearts. God alone can search the human heart and know what a person's motives really are (1 Chron. 28:9; Jer. 17:10; Rom. 8:27; Heb. 4:12).

David's occupation—a shepherd (1 Sam. 16:11). So insignificant was David in the family that Jesse didn't even call him from the flock to the feast![1] Saul was hiding among the baggage when Samuel called for him, but David was busy caring for his father's sheep. In Old Testament times, kings and their officers were looked upon as "shepherds" of the people (see Jer. 23; Ezek. 34), and David was a man with the heart of a shepherd (see 2 Sam. 7:8; 1 Chron. 21:17; Ps. 78:70-72). God's church today is a flock, and each spiritual leader needs to have the heart of a shepherd and lovingly care for God's lambs and sheep (John 10:1-18; 21:15-19; 1 Peter 5).

You can drive cattle but you have to lead sheep or they will scatter. The shepherd must know his sheep individually, love them, and take care of them according to their needs. For the most part, sheep are defenseless and do not see well, so they depend on the shepherd to guide and protect them. Though David was a literal shepherd who was called to be a "national" shepherd, he saw himself as one of the Lord's sheep and wrote about it in Psalm 23. This psalm wasn't the product of a young man but of a seasoned saint who looked back at a long life and confessed that the Lord had been faithful to him all the days of his life (23:6). David was exactly the kind of leader Israel needed to repair all the damage that Saul had done to the nation.[2]

God calls people who are busy, not people looking for ways to avoid responsibility. Moses (Ex. 3), Gideon (Jud. 6), Elisha (1 Kings 19:19-21), Nehemiah (Neh. 1), Amos (Amos 7:14-15), Peter, Andrew, James, and John (Mark 1:16-20), and Matthew (Matt. 9:9-13) were all busy when the Lord called them. God's pattern for leadership is stated in Matthew 25:21—"Well done, good and faithful servant; you were faithful over a few things, I will make you ruler over many things. Enter into the joy of your Lord" (NKJV). David had been faithful as a servant over a few things and God promoted him to being a ruler over many things—from a flock to a whole nation! Unlike Saul, David could be trusted with exercising authority because he had been under authority and had proved himself faithful.

David's appearance (1 Sam. 16:12a; see 17:42). While the physical appearance wasn't the most important thing for a king (16:7), David was so striking in his appearance that the Lord calls our attention to it. Saul was different from most Semitic people of that day because he was tall, but David's distinctive was that he was fair rather than swarthy. The word translated "ruddy" is the same as Esau's nickname "Edom—red" (Gen. 25:24-34). Some have interpreted this to mean that David was a redhead, but it may only mean that, unlike the average Semite, he was fair of skin and hair. Like Joseph, he was handsome (39:6) and had a winsome personality (1 Sam. 16:18). He was the kind of person who attracted people and won and held their confidence.

David's anointing (1 Sam. 16:12a-13). After looking at Jesse's seven sons, Samuel at last found the man of God's choice, a man after God's own heart (13:14). It's interesting that David ("beloved") was number eight, because in Scripture eight is often the number of a new beginning. God did use David to bring a new beginning to Israel, both governmentally and spiritually.[3]

In Scripture, only prophets, priests, and kings were anointed, and the anointing had to be performed by a person authorized by the Lord. In biblical imagery, oil can symbolize the Holy Spirit and the endowment of His power upon His servants (Zech. 4). The Hebrew word "Messiah" and the Greek word "Christ" both mean "anointed." The Spirit of God came upon young David in great power, and ever after that, David was God's man, but at the same time, the Spirit of God departed from Saul (1 Sam. 16:14).[4] Without the power of the Spirit, the servant of God is helpless to do the will of God and glorify Christ. As we abide in Christ, we receive the power we need, for Jesus said, "Without Me you can do nothing" (John 15:5, NKJV).

How much did David's father and brothers understand about this anointing? In view of David's subsequent association with King Saul, perhaps they interpreted the event as a consecration for David's special service to the king. It's likely that Samuel privately told David that he had been chosen by the Lord to be the next king. If so, his behavior while serving Saul was remarkably mature for a young man who one day would wear the crown. No doubt it was the assurance of this future hope that helped to keep David faithful during the ensuing years of trial and persecution.[5] But his trials and testings during those wilderness years helped to build his faith and develop his godly character and prepare him for the ministry that God had planned for him.

When David and Jonathan became friends (1 Sam. 18:1) and covenanted to be faithful to each other (18:3; 20:16), it's certain that David revealed to Jonathan that he was God's anointed king. When David became king, he would make Jonathan second in command (23:16-18). It's not likely that Jonathan told his paranoid father about David or their covenant, but somehow Saul discovered that David was his successor (20:30-31) and tried all the more to kill him. He expected his men to inform him about David and his whereabouts and Saul let them know that David was chosen to be the next king (22:6-8).

2. God prepared David (1 Sam. 16:14-23)

David knew that the Lord had been present at his conception and had arranged for his genetic structure (Ps. 139:13-16). He ordained that David would be strong and handsome, that he would possess musical talent, that he would be prudent and brave. Just as Paul was a vessel prepared by God for a specific work (Gal. 1:15; Acts 9:15), so David was God's prepared servant to accomplish His purposes for His people.

Saul's attendants knew that something was seriously wrong with their master, and they rightly attributed it to the attacks of an evil spirit. God had permitted this spirit to trouble Saul (1 Sam. 16: 14, 23; 18:10; 19:9) as part of His discipline because of the king's rebellion. By nature, Saul was a suspicious and revengeful man, and this gave the evil spirit a beachhead for his operations (Eph. 4:25-27). The one man in the kingdom who was prepared to minister to Saul was David!

David was a poet and musician, skilled at playing the harp and composing songs. By the end of his life, he was known as "the sweet psalmist of Israel" (2 Sam. 23:1). It's unusual to find such artistic talent in a man who was also a rugged soldier and fearless general. He wrote psalms, he organized the music ministry for the temple (1 Chron. 25), and provided instruments for the musicians (23:5). From the spoils of his many battles, he provided the materials for the temple, and he longed to have the privilege of building a house for the Lord. No matter how you examine his life and abilities, you find David to be a unique individual—and he was that way because God made him that way!

It was David's musical ability that introduced him into the royal court and then he was promoted to military service. The opportunities of life matched his giftedness, and David was wise to obey the will of the Lord. Just as he refused to wear Saul's armor when facing Goliath, so he rejected that which wasn't prepared and planned for him by the Lord. "He leads me in the paths of righteousness for his name's sake" (Ps. 23:3; Eph. 2:10).

The key to David's success in life is stated in 1 Sam. 16:18— "the Lord was with him." (See 18:12, 14, 28.) This was also the secret of the success of Joseph (Gen. 39:2-3, 21, 23), Joshua (Josh. 6:27), and Samuel (1 Sam. 3:19), and it is the basis for success in the Christian life today. David knew his gifts (Rom. 12:3), he experienced the power of God in using these gifts in his daily life. He loved the Lord and worshiped Him, and he surrendered himself to do the work God had called him to do. As long as he followed the Lord, God blessed and used him for his glory.

In their original meeting, Saul loved David (1 Sam. 16:21), so he obviously didn't know that his new attendant was to be the next king of Israel. However, that love was gradually replaced by envy and then fear (18:8-9, 12, 15), until Saul was determined to kill David. Saul became David's enemy (v.19), but David never treated Saul like an enemy. David behaved wisely and tried to help Saul get over his fits of depression, but they only became worse. Without God, Saul was a total failure.

3. God guided David (1 Sam. 17:1-27)

David didn't remain in Saul's camp permanently but went back and forth between the camp and home as he was needed (v. 15, NIV). Whenever he was called to help Saul, he left his flock with a dependable man (v. 20) and hurried to the camp where now he even had his own tent (v. 54). It wasn't until after David killed Goliath that Saul took him permanently to be one of his armor-bearers (18:1-2). David was a Spirit-led man and his every decision had to be in the will of God and for the glory of God. Others might come and go as they pleased, but David was guided by the providential hand of God. We can see the guidance of God in the events reported in chapter 17.

Goliath is described as standing nine feet, nine inches tall, wearing a coat of mail that weighed 125 pounds and carrying a spear that weighed 15 pounds. He was a formidable opponent indeed. He had presented himself to the army of Israel each morning and evening for forty days, and apparently David arrived on the final day (17:16). Jesse chose just the right day to send David to the battlefield to carry food supplies to his three brothers and their commanding officer (vv. 17-18). Unlike modern armies, soldiers in ancient armies had to provide their own rations and help provide for others.

David was up very early that day and heard the morning challenge that Goliath gave to Saul and his army. If the Israelites could provide a champion who was able to defeat Goliath, the Philistines would submit to the Jews and be their servants, but if not, the Israelites must consider themselves defeated and become the servants of the Philistines (vv. 8-9). Unfortunately, nobody in the Jewish army volunteered, including King Saul, who stood head and shoulders above his men. Since Israel had come to a crisis in this confrontation, Saul made a generous offer to the man who would silence Goliath: he would marry one of the king's daughters, receive great riches from the king, and take his father's house off the tax rolls. Saul hoped that somebody would be tempted by the offer and try to defeat Goliath.

David's response to Goliath's arrogant speech was that of total disgust. Who was this uncircumcised Philistine to blaspheme the name of the God of Israel? Keep in mind that David was too young to serve in the army, but he was acting as though anybody in the camp who had faith in Jehovah could challenge Goliath and defeat him! But all he saw were men fleeing from the field at the very sight of the giant, and even King Saul was terrified (vv. 11, 24).[6] God had brought David to the camp for such a time as this, and he was ready to accept the challenge.

4. God encouraged David (1 Sam. 17:28-39)

Whenever you step out by faith to fight the enemy, there's always somebody around to discourage you, and often it begins in your own home. David's eldest brother Eliab became angry when he heard that David was inquiring about Saul's offer and he ridiculed him (vv. 28-30). "We're soldiers and all you are is a shepherd boy! You came to see the battle! Go home and take care of your little flock and leave the fighting to us!" Of course, the fact that there had been no battle didn't embarrass Eliab, and he also forgot that David had originally come in order to deliver food for him, Abinadab, and Shammah. These three men had seen David anointed by Samuel but they didn't understand what it meant.

"[A] man's foes shall be they of his own household," promised Jesus (Matt. 10:36; see Micah 7:6), and that promise came true in David's life. It was also true in the life of Joseph, whose brothers hated him, lied about him, and sold him for a slave. Moses was criticized by his own brother and sister (Num. 12), and our Lord's earthly family at one time misunderstood Him and opposed His ministry (Mark 3:31-35; John 7:1-10). But David didn't allow Eliab's harsh words to discourage him, for he knew that God could help him defeat the giant.

But King Saul wasn't any more help, either in what he said or what he advised. "You are not able to go against this Philistine to fight with him; for you are but a youth, and he is a man of war from his youth" (1 Sam. 17:33, NKJV). Saul was echoing the report of the ten unbelieving spies who saw the giants in Canaan and decided that it was impossible to enter the land (Num. 13:28-29). When we walk by sight, we calculate everything from the human perspective, and this always leads to discouragement; but when we walk by faith, God comes into the equation, and that changes the results.

David had experienced the power of God in his own life and he knew that the Lord could turn weakness into power. While caring for the sheep, David had killed a lion and a bear, and he knew that the Lord could deliver him out of the hand of Goliath.

It's as though he sees Goliath as just another animal attacking God's flock! Saul knew nothing personally about this wonderful power of God, so he advised David to wear his armor. Saul didn't have the faith to believe that God could do something new, so he suggested the old-fashioned time-honored method of warfare. King Saul was a grown man and a large one at that, and David was only a teenager, so imagine what the armor looked like on David's body! But men and women of faith obey God no matter what the experts say.

David's encouragement came from God, and this is one of the secrets of his life. "But David encouraged himself in the Lord his God" (1 Sam. 30:6). In spite of criticism and in spite of discouraging counsel and bad advice, David trusted the Lord his God, and God rewarded his faith.

5. God enabled David (1 Sam. 17:40-58)

"All God's giants have been weak men, who did great things for God because they reckoned on His being with them." James Hudson Taylor, the founder of the China Inland Mission, wrote those words, but even more, he lived them. "I am the very little servant of an illustrious Master," he told a congregation in Australia. David understood what this meant, for he was but a teenager when he faced the giant; yet he knew that the Lord would be with him.

It was the Lord's victory (1 Sam. 17:40-47). It's unfortunate that this dramatic account is considered primarily a children's story or the basis for an allegory about defeating the "giants" in our lives. While there are many applications of a Bible passage, there is only one basic interpretation, and the interpretation here is that David did what he did for the glory of God. David came to the contest in the name of the Lord, the God of the armies of Israel, and he wanted Goliath, the Philistine army, and all the earth to know that the true and living God was Israel's God (v. 46). Goliath had ridiculed Israel's God and blasphemed His name, but David was about to set the record straight. David saw this as a contest between the true God of Israel and the false gods of the Philistines.

God wants to use His people to magnify His name to all the nations of the earth. This purpose was involved in the call of Abraham (Gen. 12:1-3) and God's choice of the people of Israel (Deut. 28:9-10). One purpose for Israel's sojourn in Egypt and the judgments God sent against Pharaoh was the proclaiming of God's name and glory to all the earth (Ex. 9:16). The parting of the Red Sea to let Israel out, and the opening up of the Jordan River to let them into Canaan, bore witness to all the nations that Israel's God was the true God (Josh. 4:23-24). Even the building of the temple was a witness to the Gentile nations of Israel's God so that they might know Him and fear Him (1 Kings 8:42-43). What the Lord did through David would be recorded and told around the world and bring great honor to the name of the Lord.

The very weapon that David used—a sling—was a shepherd's weapon, almost the toy of a child, and yet God used it to defeat the giant and rout the Philistine army. When Goliath saw a lad coming with a sling in one hand and a staff in the other, he laughed at him. "Am I a dog that you come at me with a stick?" But David announced that his real power was the name of the Lord of Hosts, the name that Goliath and the Philistines had insulted. David wanted the whole assembly—Israel and the Philistines—to know that the Lord doesn't need swords and spears but can deliver His people in His own way through the humblest of means. No wonder David and Jonathan became such fast friends, for they both had faith in a mighty God and wanted to fight His battles to glorify Him (1 Sam. 13:6; Pss. 33:16-22; 44:6-8).

It was David's victory (1 Sam. 17:48-51a). The Lord uses means to accomplish His purposes, and David was the prepared servant for this occasion. As a shepherd alone in the fields, he had learned to trust God, and as a faithful guardian of the flock, he had mastered the use of the sling. David had confident faith in God because he had found Him dependable in the crises of life, and he knew that the Lord would not desert him now. The Spirit of God lived in David's body and would enable him to win the battle. God guided the stone and it sank into the giant's forehead and he fell on his face before the two armies.[7] David stood over the fallen giant, took out the giant's sword, and cut off his head, an act that not only guaranteed the victim's death but also humiliated him and his army and announced total victory. Years later, David would write, "It is God who arms me with strength, and makes my way perfect. . . . He teaches my hands to make war so that my arms can bend a bow of bronze" (Ps. 18:32, 34, NKJV).

It became Israel's victory (1 Sam. 17:51b-54). Even as a youth, David displayed one of the marks of a great leader: he took the risk and opened the way so that others could share in the victory. The Philistines didn't keep their part of the bargain and submit to Israel (v. 9); instead, they fled in fear, so the Jews chased them at least ten miles to the cities of Gath (Goliath's hometown, v. 4) and Ekron, slaying the enemy soldiers all the way.[8] It turned out to be a tremendous victory for Saul's army. When the Israelites returned to the Philistine camp, they claimed the spoils of the victory that the Lord and David had won. David apparently accompanied the men in chasing the enemy (v. 57) and began to get the reputation of being a brave soldier (18:7). He stripped the giant and took his armor and put it in his tent. Later Goliath's sword will show up with the Jewish priests in Nob (21:1-9), so David must have dedicated it to the Lord by giving it to the priests.

When did David take Goliath's head to Jerusalem? Probably later when he conquered the city and made it his capital (2 Sam. 5:1-10). The city was known as Jebus in that day and was inhabited by the Jebusites (Jud. 19:10), so this verse was written into the text later when the name had been changed. When David moved into the city as king, he no doubt brought with him many precious trophies from his battles. The head of Goliath, as grisly as it was, would remind David that the Lord could be trusted to give the victory if we seek only to glorify Him.

It was not Saul's victory (1 Sam. 17:55-58). When Jonathan attacked the Philistine outpost (14:1-23), Saul was a spectator, and his bad decisions almost cost them a victory; and once again,

Saul merely watched as David defeated the enemy single-handed. This would be Saul's pattern of leadership to the tragic end of his life.

Saul knew who David was, but he asked Abner who the lad's father was, for in that day, that was how people were identified. Jesse had been mentioned earlier in Saul's circle (16:18) but perhaps Abner wasn't present and Saul may easily have forgotten. (Do we know the names of our acquaintances' fathers?) As Saul's minstrel, David went back and forth between home and the camp, and he was present only when Saul was oppressed by the evil spirit; so we can excuse Saul for not knowing who Jesse was. The fact that the victor's family was relieved of paying taxes, and he would marry Saul's daughter was part of the bargain (17:25), so Saul would have to inquire about the father. Finally, Saul may have wanted to know if there were any more men like David back home. He probably didn't know that three of David's brothers were in his army, but he could have used a few more men like David! (See 14:52.) The result of the day's victory was that David was added permanently to Saul's staff.

It has well been said that there are people who make things happen, people who watch things happen and people who don't know that anything is happening. David had insight into Israel's plight and knew what was happening. He realized that it wasn't a physical conflict between two armies, but a spiritual battle between truth and error, faith and superstition, the true and living God and dead idols. David's faith lifted the war to a much higher plane, just as Paul did in Ephesians 6:10ff. Our battle is against the devil and his army, and human weapons are useless in that conflict.

Faith in God makes us participants with the Lord in the battle for truth. "And this is the victory that has overcome the world—our faith" (1 John 5:4). [9]

SEVEN

A Jealous King

Jewish men had to be at least twenty years old before they could go to war (Num. 1:3), but David was probably only eighteen when he was made a high-ranking officer in the Jewish army (18:5, NIV). From the beginning of his new assignment, David found himself in a life-threatening conflict with King Saul. David didn't *create* problems for Saul; he *revealed* the deep-seated problems that were already there. David was an honest man of faith, but Saul was a deceitful, scheming man of the world. With great humility David had accepted his appointment as Israel's next king, while Saul was almost paranoid as he tried to protect his throne. God had abandoned Saul but had given His Spirit's power to David, and David moved from victory to victory as he led Saul's troops. We can trace some of the major stages in Saul's growing opposition to David.

1. Saul wants David killed (1 Sam. 18:1-12)

At one time, Saul loved David (16:21, "liked him very much," NIV), but the king's attitude changed into jealousy and then hatred. The Lord was with David (18:12, 14, 28), however, and Saul was not permitted to harm him. During the ten years or so that David was a fugitive, the Lord not only thwarted Saul's plans repeatedly, but He even used the king's hostility to mature David and make him into a man of courage and faith. While Saul was guarding his throne, David was being prepared for his throne.

Love (1 Sam. 18:1-4). Too many Bible readers still view David and Jonathan as two frolicsome teenagers who liked each other because they had many common interests, but this picture is shallow and inaccurate. Jonathan had to be at least twenty years old to be in his father's army, and the fact that Jonathan was already commanding one-third of that army and had won two great victories (13:1-4; 14:1ff) indicates that he was a seasoned soldier and not a callow adolescent. Some biblical chronologists calculate that there could have been an age difference of twenty-five to twenty-eight years between David and Jonathan.

Jonathan listened to his father and David converse, and after that interview, took David to his own heart with the kind of manly affection that comrades in arms understand.[1] Jonathan was Saul's eldest son, destined for the throne of Israel, and the Lord had already given it to David, so their friendship was certainly unique. When Jonathan gave his official garments and his armor to David, making him a friend and equal, Jonathan was acknowledging that David would one day take his place, so David must have told Jonathan about his anointing. The two friends covenanted that when David became king, Jonathan would be second in command (20:16-17, 42; 23:16-18), and David covenanted to protect Jonathan's family from being slain.

Saul wasn't pleased with his son's friendship with David. For one thing, Jonathan was Saul's best commander and was needed to make the king look good. Saul was also afraid that Jonathan would divulge court secrets to David, and when Saul discovered that David was already anointed to succeed him, this made matters worse. He saw David as an enemy, a threat to his own son's future, although Jonathan didn't view it that way. But when a leader nurtures himself on pride, jealousy and fear, he suspects everybody.

Popularity (1 Sam. 18:5-7). "The crucible for silver and the furnace for gold, but a man is tested by the praise he receives" (Prov. 27:21, NIV). Just as the crucible and furnace test the metal and prepare it for use, so praise tests and prepares people for what God has planned for them. How we respond to praise reveals what we're made of and whether or not we're ready to take on new responsibilities. If praise humbles us, then God can use us, but if praise puffs us up, we're not yet ready for a promotion.

In his attitudes, conduct, and service, David was a complete success, and Saul's servants and the Jewish people recognized this and praised him publicly. This popular acclaim started after David's stunning defeat of Goliath, when the army of Israel chased the Philistines for ten miles, defeated them, and took their spoils (1 Sam. 17:52ff). As Saul and his men returned to camp, the women met the victors and praised both Saul and David. In true Hebrew fashion, their praise was exaggerated, but in one sense it was true. David's victory over Goliath made it possible for the whole army of Israel to conquer the Philistines, so each soldier's achievement was really a triumph for David.

Envy and anger (1 Sam. 18:8-11). "It is a dangerous crisis when a proud heart meets with flattering lips," said John Flavel, seventeenth-century British Presbyterian clergyman and author. What the women sang didn't seem to affect David, but their song enraged Saul. Saul had already forfeited the kingdom (15:28), but he still asked, "What can he have more but the kingdom?" Saul's response to David's success was exactly opposite that of John the Baptist when he was told of the great success of Jesus: "He must increase, but I must decrease" (John 3:30).

Envy is a dangerous and insidious enemy, a cancer that slowly eats out our inner life and leads us to say and do terrible things. Proverbs 14:30 rightly calls it "the rottenness of the bones." Envy is the pain we feel within when somebody achieves or receives what we think belongs to us. Envy is the sin of successful people who can't stand to see others reach the heights they have reached and eventually replace them. By nature, we are proud and want to be recognized and applauded; and from childhood we have been taught to compete with others. Dr. Bob Cook often reminded us that everybody wears a sign that reads, "Please make me feel important." Much modern advertising thrives on envy as it cleverly contrasts the "haves" and the "have-nots" and urges the "have-nots" to buy the latest products and keep up with the "haves." Envious people max out their credit cards to buy things they don't need just to impress people who really don't care!

But envy easily leads to anger, and anger is often the first step toward murder (Matt. 5:21-26). This explains why Saul threw his spear at David while David was trying to soothe the king and help him overcome his depression. The Lord enabled David to escape, and when he returned to the king a second time, Saul only tried again to kill him. These two events probably occurred after the Goliath victory but before David was made an officer in the army, and yet David remained faithful to his king.

Fear (v. 12). The Lord protected His servant David from Saul's murderous hand, a fact that frightened Saul even more (vv. 15, 29). Surely Saul knew he was fighting a losing battle, for the Lord was on David's side but had departed from him. However, Saul kept up a brave front as he tried to impress his officers with his authority. Even if Saul missed his target, the people around him didn't miss the message he was sending: "Saul is king and he wants David to be killed."

2. Saul plots to have David killed (1 Sam. 18:13-30)

"Faith is living without scheming," but Saul was better at scheming than at trusting God. If Saul disobeyed God, he always had a ready excuse to get himself out of trouble, and if people challenged his leadership, he could figure out ways to eliminate them. Possessed by anger and envy, and determined to hold on to his crown, Saul decided that young David had to be killed.

Saul sends David into battle (1 Sam. 18:13-16). Since David was an excellent soldier and a born leader, the logical thing was to give him assignments that would take him away from the camp where the enemy could kill him. Saul made David commander over 1,000 and sent him to fight the Philistines. If David was killed in battle, it was the enemy's fault; and if he lost a battle but lived, his popularity would wane. But the plan didn't work because David won all the battles! After all, the Lord was with him and the power of God was upon him. Instead of eliminating David or diminishing his popularity, Saul's scheme only made him a greater hero to the people, and this increased Saul's fear of David all the more.

Saul demands an impossible feat (1 Sam. 18:17-27). Saul had promised to give one of his daughters in marriage to the man who killed Goliath (17:25), but this promise had not yet been fulfilled. The fact that David had killed Goliath wasn't enough, for Saul now expected David to "fight the battles of the Lord" in order to gain his wife, Saul's eldest daughter Merab. Saul wasn't beneath using his own daughter as a tool to get rid of David. The details aren't given, but it seems that David had to fight a certain number of battles before the marriage could take place. Of course, the king was hoping that David would be slain during one of those battles, and then Saul would lose his enemy but still have his daughter. However, David humbly declined the offer, saying that his family wasn't worthy to be related to the king; so Saul gave Merab to another suitor.[2]

Then Saul happily discovered that his younger daughter Michal was in love with David! Saul spoke to David about it and said he would give him a second chance to claim his reward. Once again David demurred, but Saul persisted. This time he asked selected servants to lie to David and tell him that Saul liked him and wanted him to marry Michal, and that Saul's attendants agreed with the proposal. But David put them off by telling the truth: he was from a lowly family and he didn't have any money to pay the bride price (Gen. 34:12; Ex. 22:16).

When David's reply was reported to Saul, the devious king saw in it a great opportunity to attack his enemies and get rid of David at the same time. Saul told his servants to tell David that all that the king required for a bride price was 100 foreskins from the "uncircumcised Philistines." Saul was certain that at some point in this endeavor, David would meet his death. Once again, Saul was using one of his daughters to help destroy an innocent man, and in this instance, it was a man she truly loved.

Whether the phrase "the appointed days" (1 Sam. 18:26) refers to a new deadline or the original deadline determined by Saul for Merab is really unimportant, because David and his men[3] accomplished even more than Saul had asked. David once more survived the battles and he brought the king 200 foreskins. Another of Saul's schemes had failed and he had to give Michal to David as his wife.

Saul is even more afraid (1 Sam. 18:28-30). We have seen this pattern before (vv. 12, 15), but now Saul's twisted emotions so controlled him that he was obsessed with the desire to kill his son-in-law. David never considered Saul to be his enemy (Ps. 18 inscription), but Saul remained David's enemy until the day he died on the battlefield. David continued to fight the Lord's battles, and the Lord continued to give him great success and to magnify his name above the names of Saul's best officers. David certainly paid close attention to what God was doing in him and for him, and no doubt the remembrance of these events encouraged him during the difficult days of his exile. "If God be for us, who can be against us?" (Rom. 8:31)

3. Saul looks for opportunities to have David killed (1 Sam. 19:1-17)
Saul's mind and heart were so possessed by hatred for David that he openly admitted to Jonathan and the court attendants that he intended to have his son-in-law killed. Saul was now through with behind-the-scenes plots and was out to destroy David the quickest way possible, and he ordered Jonathan and the royal attendants to join him in his endeavor. The hope of Israel lay in the heart and ministry of David, and yet Saul wanted to kill him! David would conquer Israel's enemies and consolidate the kingdom. He would gather much of the wealth used to build the temple. He would write psalms for the Levites to sing in praising God, and he would even design the musical instruments they played. God's covenant with David would keep the light shining in Jerusalem during the dark days of the nation's decline, and the fulfillment of that covenant would bring Jesus Christ the Messiah

into the world. No wonder Satan was so determined to kill David!

Jonathan's intervention (1 Sam. 19:1-10). Surely Saul knew that Jonathan would pass the word along to his beloved friend David, but perhaps that's what the king desired. If he couldn't kill David, perhaps he could so frighten him that he would leave the land and never be seen again. Jonathan did report the king's words to David and suggested that his friend hide in the field the next morning when Jonathan would speak with his father on behalf of David. It's remarkable that such a magnificent son could belong to such a wicked father! Had Jonathan been a self-ish man, he could have helped to eliminate David and secure the crown for himself, but he submitted to the will of God and assisted David.

Jonathan presented his father with two arguments: (1) David was an innocent man who was not deserving of death,[4] and (2) David had served Saul faithfully by winning great victories against Israel's enemies. David was a valuable man to have around and he had never sinned against the king. Jonathan didn't mention that David was also very popular with the soldiers and the common people, because making such a statement would only have aroused the king's anger and envy. Saul was enjoying a sane moment and agreed with his son, and even took an oath not to kill David. Saul was a liar and his oaths were meaningless (14:24, 44), but this did open the way for David to return to court.

When the Philistines attacked Israel again, David went out with his men and soundly defeated them. This only aroused Saul's envy and anger and once again he tried to pin David to the wall (18:10-11). Satan is a liar and a murderer (John 8:44), and because Saul was controlled by the evil one, he broke his oath and he threw his spear. David knew that the time had come for him to leave Saul's presence and hide, but first he went home to see his wife Michal. David would now begin about ten years of exile during which God would make a leader out of him.

Michal's deception (1 Sam. 19:11-17). Saul surmised that David would go home, so he sent men that night to watch David's house and kill him when he came out the next morning. Knowing her father's thought processes, Michal urged David to get out that night and flee to a place of safety. She let him down through a window and arranged a dummy in the bed by using an idol and some goats' hair. What Michal was doing with an pagan idol (teraphim) is a mystery, especially one as large as a man. (Rachel hid two teraphim under a saddle—Gen. 31:33-35.) It's possible that the idol was only a bust and that she used it and the goats' hair[5] for the head and used pillows to simulate the body. Michal was still depending on idols while married to a man after God's own heart, and like her father, she was a schemer.

While Michal was scheming, David was praying and trusting the Lord, and Psalm 59 came out of this experience. As you read this psalm, you see Saul's spies running here and there and waiting for David to emerge from his house, and you hear David comparing them to snarling dogs lurking in the city streets. But David's faith was in the Lord, for only the Lord could be his defense and his refuge. This doesn't mean that David rejected any plans for escape, because the Lord uses human means to accomplish His divine ends; but it does mean that David's faith was not in himself or in Michal's schemes, but in the Lord of the armies of Israel.

In the morning, when the agents demanded that Michal surrender her husband, she told them he was sick, and when they reported this to Saul, he told the men to bring him David, bed and all! But when they picked up the bed, the truth was revealed, and Michal was reproved by her father for being so deceptive, but she was only following his example! Like her father, she lied and claimed that David had threatened to kill her if she didn't cooperate.

4. Saul himself goes to kill David (1 Sam. 19:18-24)

David fled to Samuel in Ramah, a godly friend he knew he could depend on, and Samuel took him to the fellowship of the prophets where they could worship God and seek His face. The word *naioth* means "dwellings" and was probably a section in

Ramah where the "school of the prophets" assembled. There Samuel and David could worship and pray and ask God for wisdom, and the prophets would pray with them. But Saul's spies were everywhere and they reported to Saul where he could find David. The king sent three different groups of soldiers to capture David, but when they arrived at the place where the prophets had assembled, they were immediately possessed by the Spirit and began to praise and worship God! The Hebrew word translated "prophesy" can mean "to sing songs and praise God" as well as "to foretell events." Saul's soldiers didn't become prophets; they only uttered words inspired by the Spirit of God. God protected David and Samuel, not by sending an army but by sending the Holy Spirit to turn warriors into worshipers. "The weapons we fight with are not the weapons of the world. On the contrary, they have divine power to demolish strongholds" (2 Cor. 10:4, NIV).

Three groups of soldiers had failed, so Saul decided to go to Ramah himself. David's presence in Ramah was no secret because the people at the great cistern knew where he and Samuel were and they told Saul. Perhaps the entire town knew that some kind of "spiritual revival" was taking place at the school of the prophets. Saul hastened to the place only to be met by the Spirit of God and made to praise the Lord. He took off his outer royal garments and became like any other man, and he lay on the floor before Samuel. This would be their last meeting until that fateful night when Samuel came from the realms of the dead to pass judgment on the king (1 Sam. 28:7ff).

But Saul had had a similar experience after Samuel had anointed him king (10:9-13), and from it came the proverbial saying, "Is Saul also among the prophets?" After Saul's experience at Ramah, the proverb was resurrected. These two events prove that a person can have a remarkable religious experience and yet have no change in character. In Saul's case, both experiences were actually sent by the Lord, but Saul didn't profit from them. Special religious manifestations aren't evidences that a person is even saved (Matt. 7:21-23). Judas preached sermons and even performed miracles (Matt. 10:1-8), yet he was not a believer (John 6:67-71; 13:10-11; 17:12), and he betrayed the Lord and ended up committing suicide. Saul, like Judas, had many opportunities to see the Lord's hand at work, and yet he never had a life-changing experience with the Lord.

While Saul was occupied at the school of the prophets, David slipped away from Ramah and went to meet Jonathan somewhere near Gibeah. David and Jonathan would make one final effort at reconciliation with Saul, and it would almost cost Jonathan his life. Saul was a "double-minded man, unstable in all his ways" (James 1:8, NKJV). He would try to rule the land and defeat the Philistines while at the same time chasing David and seeking to kill him. The longer David eluded him, the more fanatical Saul became, until finally he ended his own life on the battlefield, lacking the help of the one man who could have given him victory.

EIGHT

David in Exile

David has been criticized and called impulsive because he left Ramah and his friend Samuel and fled to Gibeah to confer with Jonathan. But David knew that Saul's ecstatic experience would soon end and would leave his heart unchanged. Saul had promised Jonathan that he wouldn't kill David (19:6), but he had already broken that promise four times (vv. 20-24), so the wisest course for David was to get away from Saul and go into hiding. For David to remain at Gibeah wasn't an exercise of faith; it was an act of presumption and he was only tempting God. The drama in these three chapters involves four persons: Jonathan, Saul, David, and Doeg.

1. Jonathan—a faithful friend (1 Sam. 20:1-23)

In all literature, David and Jonathan stand out as examples of devoted friends. Jonathan had the more difficult situation because he wanted to be loyal to his father while at the same time being a friend to the next king of Israel. Conflict of loyalties, especially in the family, is one of the most painful difficulties we face in the life of faith (Matt. 10:34-39), but Christ calls for supreme devotion to Him and His will for our lives.

Conferring (1 Sam. 20:1-10, 18-23). David met Jonathan somewhere near Gibeah and wasted no time confronting his beloved friend with the key question: "What have I done that is so evil that your father wants to kill me?" David hadn't disobeyed any royal commands, incited any rebellion against the throne, or broken God's law, yet Saul was bent on destroying him.[1] David knew that Saul was an envious man who wanted to keep the throne for himself and hand it on to his descendants, but David had faith that the Lord would remove Saul from the scene in His good time and in His own way (26:7-11). David dearly loved Jonathan and didn't want to hurt him by criticizing his father, but now it was a matter of life or death.

Jonathan's reply sounds rather naïve, especially in the light of Saul's statement in 19:1 and his behavior at Ramah. Saul had thrown his spear at David at least three times (10–11; 19:9-10), and he had sent three groups of soldiers to capture him, and Saul finally went to Ramah himself to do the job (vv. 20-24). How much evidence did Jonathan need that his father was a disturbed man out to destroy God's anointed king? Jonathan mistakenly thought that his own relationship to his father was closer than it really was and that Saul would confide in him, but subsequent events proved him wrong, for Saul would even try to kill Jonathan!

David refuted Jonathan's argument by stating that the logical thing for Saul to do was to keep his eldest son in the dark. Saul knew that David and Jonathan were devoted friends and that Jonathan would be pained if he knew Saul's real intentions. The matter was so serious that David couldn't put his faith in what Saul told Jonathan. "There is but a step between me and death" (20:3). This was true both metaphorically and literally, for three times David had dodged the king's spear.

Jonathan offered to help in any way his friend suggested, and David proposed a simple test of Saul's true feelings. It was customary for each Jewish family to hold a feast at the new moon (Num. 10:10; 28:11-15; Ps. 81:3), and Saul would expect David to attend. If Saul's son-in-law and leading military hero didn't attend the feast, it would be an insult to the king as well as the family, so David's absence would help reveal Saul's genuine attitude toward David. If Saul became angry, then David's assessment was correct, but if Saul excused David and didn't press the matter, then Jonathan was correct. The only problem with this scheme was that it required Jonathan to lie by saying that David had gone to Bethlehem to attend his own family's feast. David would be hiding in the field and waiting for Jonathan to tell him whether or not it was safe to come home.[2]

How would Jonathan safely get the message to David? (1 Sam. 20: 10) He couldn't trust one of the servants to carry the word, so, in spite of the danger, he would have to do it himself. He devised a simple plan involving shooting three arrows out in the field where David was hiding (v. 20). Jonathan would call to the lad who was helping him and in this way signal David and tell him what to do. Even if some of Saul's spies were present, they wouldn't understand what was going on.

Covenanting (1 Sam. 20:11-17). From verse 11 to verse 23, David is silent while Jonathan reviews the covenant they had made with each other (18:1-4). Jonathan even took an oath and promised to give David the correct message on the third day of the feast, so he would know whether the king was friendly or angry.[3] Jonathan went beyond the immediate crisis to deal with future events. He knew that David would one day become king, and he prayed that the Lord would bless his reign. In their covenant, they agreed that Jonathan would serve next to David as second in command (23:16-18), and now Jonathan asked that if anything happened to him, David would promise not to wipe out his household, and David agreed. The phrase "the kindness of the Lord" (20:14) shows up in 2 Samuel 9 where David's compassionate care of Jonathan's crippled son, Mephibosheth, is described.

Jonathan reaffirmed his oath and included the whole house of David (1 Sam. 20:16), and he asked David to repeat his covenant oath as well. There's no mention of the offering of a covenant sacrifice (Gen. 15) or the signing of a covenant document, because the love the two men had for the Lord and each other was sufficient to make the agreement binding. Jonathan had brought much joy and encouragement to David during those difficult years, but it wasn't God's will that David permanently join himself to Saul and his family, for they belonged to the wrong tribe and represented a rejected and condemned monarchy. David never had a co-regent because Jonathan was killed in battle (1 Sam. 31:1-2), and David rejected Saul's daughter Michal as his wife and she died childless (2 Sam. 6:16-23). Had she borne any children, it would have brought confusion into the royal line.

2. Saul—a spiteful king (1 Sam. 20:24-42)

On the first day of the feast, David hid himself by the stone of Ezel and waited for Jonathan's signal, for it was remotely possible that the king might be favorably inclined and welcome him back into the official circle.

David's absence (1 Sam. 20:24-29). Constantly afraid of personal attack, Saul sat with his back to the wall, his commander Abner next to him, and Jonathan across from his father. David's place next to Jonathan was empty, but the king said nothing about it, convinced that David was ceremonially unclean and therefore unable to eat a holy feast that day. The feast consisted primarily of meat from the new moon fellowship offerings, and anyone ceremonially unclean was prohibited from participating (Lev. 7:20-21). Perhaps David had touched something unclean, or he may have had intercourse with his wife (15:16-18). If so, all he had to do was separate himself from other people for that day, bathe his body, and change clothes, and he could come back into society the next day.

But when the men met for their meal the second day, again David was missing, which suggested to Saul that his son-in-law's absence was caused by something more serious than simple ritual defilement. An unclean person could remove the defilement in a day, but David had been missing for two days. Suspicious of anything out of the ordinary in his official staff, Saul asked

Jonathan why David was absent, disdainfully calling him "the son of Jesse" rather than by his given name that was now so famous. Later, Saul would try to humiliate the high priest Ahimelech by calling him "the son of Ahitub" (1 Sam. 22:11-12).

At this point Jonathan dropped his lie into the conversation and nothing went right after that. Jonathan didn't say that David's father Jesse had summoned him home but that one of his brothers had *commanded* him to attend the family feast. Perhaps Jonathan hoped his father would assume that the invitation came from one of David's three brothers serving in Saul's army (17:13), which might make the matter easier for Saul to accept. Jonathan also used a verb that means "to get away, to make a quick visit" so that Saul wouldn't suspect David of going home for a long visit and rallying his own troops so he could seize the throne.

Saul's anger (1 Sam. 20:30-34). When hateful feelings are in the heart, it doesn't take much for angry words to come out of the mouth (Matt. 12:34-35). Saul had probably been brooding over how David had insulted him by refusing to attend the feast, and the longer to brooded, the more the fire raged within. But instead of attacking David, King Saul attacked his own son! Had the Lord not intervened back in Ramah, Saul would have killed David in the very presence of the Prophet Samuel (1 Sam. 19:22-24), and now he reviled his own son while eating a holy feast!

The king's tirade seems to disparage his own wife, but rightly understood, his words describe his son as the lowest of the low. According to Saul, Jonathan's treachery in befriending David indicated that he was not Saul's son at all but the son of some other man, for a son of Saul would never betray his father. Therefore, Jonathan was slandering his own mother and saying she was a common prostitute, a rebel against the Law of Moses, and a woman who practiced perversion. Because Jonathan helped David and didn't protect his father's throne, he had shamed his mother as much as if he had exposed her nakedness. She bore him to be the successor to his father, and now Jonathan had refused the crown in favor of the son of Jesse. The king was shouting, "You are no son of mine! You must be illegitimate!"

Saul's great concern was the preservation of the kingdom *that the Lord had already taken from him.* God had made it very clear that none of Saul's sons would ever inherit the throne and David was the king of God's choice, so Saul was fighting the will of God and asking Jonathan to do the same thing. Saul was aware that his son knew where David was hiding and commanded Jonathan to find David and bring him in to be slain. When Jonathan remonstrated with his father and refused to obey the royal command, Saul threw his spear at his own son! Jonathan left the table in great anger and spent the rest of the day fasting.

Jonathan's alarm (1 Ssam. 20:35-42). Jonathan waited until the next day and then went out into the field with one of his young attendants as though he were going to practice shooting arrows. As he promised David, he shot three arrows (v. 20), one of which was sent far beyond the boy, making it necessary for Jonathan to shout to the lad. But his words were meant for David's ears: "Hurry! Go quickly! Don't linger!" When the boy came back with the arrows, Jonathan gave him the bow and sent him back to the city, and then he ran out to meet David.

This was not their last meeting (23:16-18), but it was certainly a profoundly emotional farewell. They both wept, but David wept the most. He didn't know how many years of exile lay before him, and perhaps he might never see his beloved friend again. Eastern peoples aren't ashamed to weep, embrace, and kiss one another when they meet or when they part (Gen. 31:55; Acts 20:37). Jonathan's, "Go in peace" must have encouraged David. Both men reaffirmed their covenant, knowing that the Lord heard their words and saw their hearts.[4] David left and traveled three miles to the priestly city of Nob, and Jonathan returned to Gibeah and continued to be an officer in his father's army.

Ten years later, the Philistines would kill Saul, Jonathan, and his brothers on the battlefield (1 Sam. 31:1-6).

3. David—a hopeful exile (1 Sam. 21:1–22:5)

When David fled to Nob, it marked the beginning of an exile
that lasted about ten years (21:1–29:11). Not all of David's
wilderness experiences are recorded, but enough history has been
given to show us that he was a man of faith and courage. While
it's difficult to determine the background of every psalm, it's likely that David's fugitive years are reflected in Psalms 7, 11–13,
16–17, 22, 25, 31, 34–35, 52–54, 56–59, 63–64, 142–143. Psalm
18 is his song of praise when God gave him triumph over his enemies.[5] It's wonderful that David wrote so many encouraging
psalms during this period of great suffering, and from them God's
people today can find strength and courage in their own times of
testing. Our Lord quoted Psalm 22:1 and 31:5 when on the cross.

David goes to Nob (1 Sam. 21:1-9). This was a priestly town
three miles south of Gibeah where the tabernacle was located.
(The ark was still in the house of Abinadab in Kiriath Jearim;
7:1.) Because of his friendship with Samuel, David knew he
would find refuge and help among the priests there; and he had
a strong personal devotion to the sanctuary of the Lord (Ps. 27:4-
6). The fact that David arrived alone frightened Ahimelech, the
high priest, who was a great-grandson of Eli and was also known
as Ahijah (1 Sam. 14:3). He knew David's reputation and position and wondered that he was traveling without a royal
entourage.

If "the king" in 21:2 refers to the Lord Jehovah (see 20:42),
then David isn't lying, for David certainly was doing the Lord's
business and would be for the rest of his life. But if this statement
was a deliberate lie, then David was scheming instead of trusting.
His motive was probably to protect the high priest from Saul's
future investigations, but the plan failed; for Saul killed
Ahimelech and all the priests except Abiathar, because they
conspired with his enemy. However, it is possible that David had
asked some of his men to rendezvous with him at the cave of
Adullam (see 22:2). David's reference to the ritual purity of his
men suggests this.

David needed food, so Ahimelech gave him the sacred loaves

from the tabernacle, food that was reserved only for the priests (Lev. 24:5-9). If the people had been bringing their tithes to the tabernacle as the law commanded, there would have been more food available, but it was a time of spiritual decline in the land. Jesus used this incident to teach a lesson on true obedience and spiritual discernment (Matt. 12:1-8; Mark 2:23-28; Luke 6:1-5).[6]Ahimelech wanted to be sure that David's soldiers were ritually clean, and David assured him that neither the men nor their equipment had been defiled (Lev. 15:16-18). David also asked for Goliath's sword, which for some reason was kept in the tabernacle alongside the ephod (Ex. 28:4-13). David could now proceed on his journey with food to strengthen himself and a sword for protection.

Doeg's presence at the tabernacle is a mystery. He was an Edomite and therefore not born a child of the covenant, but he was "detained before the Lord" at the sanctuary (1 Sam. 21:7). Perhaps he had become a Jewish proselyte and was following the Hebrew faith in order to hold his job. As Saul's chief shepherd, Doeg could easily have become defiled so that he had to bring a sacrifice to the Lord. David knew that Doeg would report to Saul what he had seen at Nob and that this would mean trouble (22:9ff).

From Nob to Gath (1 Sam. 21:10-15). Fear of Saul now temporarily replaced faith in the Lord, and David fled twenty-three miles to the enemy city of Gath, the home of the Philistine giant Goliath (17:4). It wasn't a safe place to go, but after seeing Doeg at Nob, David may have decided that his presence anywhere in Israel would only jeopardize the lives of his friends, so he decided to leave the land. Furthermore, the last place Saul would look for him would be in Philistia. David's reputation as a great warrior had preceded him,[7] and the king and his counselors didn't view his presence as a blessing. David then pretended to be mad, and this made it easy for him to escape unharmed. Had David waited on the Lord and sought His will, he might not have gotten into trouble.

Psalms 34 and 56 both came out of this bizarre experience.

Psalm 56 was his prayer for God's help when the situation became dangerous, and Psalm 34 was his hymn of praise after God had delivered him, although he mentions "fear" (vv. 4, 7) and deliverance from trouble (1 Sam. 21:6, 17, 19). The emphasis in Psalm 56 is on the slander and verbal attacks of the Philistine leaders as they tried to get their king to deal with David. There's no question that David was a frightened man while he was in Gath, but he sustained his faith by remembering God's promises (vv. 10-11) and God's call upon his life (v. 12). According to Psalm 34, David did a lot of praying while in Gath (vv. 4-6, 17-22), and the Lord heard him. David learned that the fear of the Lord conquers every other fear (vv. 9-16). The Lord was indeed merciful to David to enable him to escape back to his own land. No matter how we feel or how dismal the circumstances appear, the safest place in the world is in the will of God.

From Gath to the cave of Adullam (1 Sam. 22:1-2). This was a well-known place in Judah, ten miles from Gath and about fifteen miles from Bethlehem, David's hometown. David was at least in friendly territory, and the fighting men from Judah and Benjamin came to join his band (1 Chron. 12:16-18). It was here that David longed for a drink of water from the well at Bethlehem and three of his mighty men broke through enemy lines to bring it to him (2 Sam. 23:13-17). Knowing how much that drink of water cost those three men who risked their lives, David poured it out as a drink offering to the Lord. Great leaders don't take their followers for granted or treat lightly the sacrifices that they make beyond the call of duty.

All of David's family joined him at the cave, which meant that his brothers deserted Saul's army and became fugitives like David. They knew that David was God's anointed king, so they linked up with the future of the nation. Many others saw in David the only hope for a successful kingdom, so they came to him as well: those who were in distress because of Saul, those in debt, and those discontented because of the way Saul was ruining the nation (see 1 Sam. 14:29). David ended up with 400 high quality fighting men, and the number later increased to 600

(23:13; 25:13; 27:2; 30:9). Some of his mighty men and their leaders are listed in 2 Sam. 23:8-39 and 1 Chron. 11:10-41. Saul had an army of 3,000 chosen men (1 Sam. 26:2).

True leaders attract the best people who see in the leader those qualities of character that they most admire. The people around David would never have been noticed in history were it not for their association with him, just as our Lord's disciples would have died unknown had they not walked with Jesus. God usually doesn't call the great and the powerful to be His servants, but those who have a heart for Him and an eagerness to obey His will (1 Cor. 1:26-31). David's little band of rejects represented the future of the nation, and God's blessing was with them. History reveals that it is the devoted remnant, small as it might be, that holds the key to the future of God's work on this earth.

Psalms 57 and 142 are associated with David's stay in the cave of Adullam, and both of them emphasize David's faith that God was his refuge. As David prayed, the cave became a holy tabernacle where by faith he could find shelter under the wings of the cherubim in the Holy of Holies (57:1). What looked like a cave to others was to David a divine sanctuary, for the Lord was his portion and his refuge (142:5). To David, the fugitive life was like being in prison (v. 7), but he trusted the Lord to see him through. He knew that God would keep his promises and give him the throne and the kingdom.

From Adullam to Moab (1 Sam. 22:3-4a). David honored his father and mother and sought to protect them, so he asked the king of Moab to shelter them until his days of exile were over. The Moabites were the descendants of Lot from his incestuous relationship with his older daughter (Gen. 19:30-38). In the days of Moses, the Moabites were not a people favored by the Jews (Deut. 23:3-6), but David's great-grandmother Ruth came from Moab (Ruth 4:18-22), and this may have helped David to gain their support.

From Adullam to "the stronghold" (1 Sam. 22:4b). After David had secured the safety of his parents, he returned to Adullam and then moved his company to "the stronghold" or "fortress," which many students believe was at Masada by the Dead Sea, about thirty-five miles southwest of Adullam. The Hebrew word *mesuda* means "fortress" or "stronghold," and can refer to natural hiding places in the wilderness. David lived in different "desert strongholds" (23:14, NIV) as he tried to protect himself and his friends and outwit Saul and his spies. But the Prophet Gad warned David that the wilderness fortress wasn't safe and that he should return to the land of Judah, so he relocated in the forest of Hereth in the vicinity of the cave of Adullam. *Hereth* means "thicket."

The Prophet Gad will appear again in the narrative of David's life. It was he who gave David the Lord's message after David had numbered the people (2 Sam. 24:11-19; 1 Chron. 21:9-19) and assisted David in setting up the musical ministry for the sanctuary of the Lord (2 Chron. 29:25). He also wrote a book about David's reign (1 Chron. 29:29). Later, Abiathar the priest would escape Saul's slaughter of the priests at Nob and join David, so that the king would have available the ministries of both prophet and priest.

4. Doeg: a deceitful servant (1 Sam. 22:6-23)

Now we discover why the writer mentioned Doeg in verse 7, for now he steps forth as a key actor in the drama. Wherever there is a scheming leader, he will have scheming followers, for we reproduce after our own kind. These are people who will do anything to gain the leader's approval and receive his rewards, and Doeg was such a man. This was the perfect time for him to use his knowledge to please the king and raise his own stature before the other officers. The fact that he was accusing God's anointed king didn't bother him, or that he lied about what the high priest said and did. It is no wonder that David despised Doeg and express his loathing in the words of Psalm 52.

The king's anger (1 Sam. 22:6-10). King Saul, spear in hand (18:10; 19:9; 26:7-22), was holding court under a tree on a hill[8] near Gibeah when word came to him that his spies[9] had discovered David's latest hiding place. This was probably the wilderness stronghold near the Dead Sea (1 Sam. 22:4-5), which explains why God sent the message to Gad that the company should return to Judah. Saul used this event as an occasion to berate his officers, all of whom were from his own tribe of Benjamin.[10] Always suspicious of treachery in the official ranks, Saul reminded the men that he was king and therefore was the only one who could reward them for their faithful service. David attracted men who were willing to risk their lives for him, but Saul had to use bribery and fear to keep his forces together. Saul was sure that his officers were conspiring against him because they had refused to tell him that David and Jonathan had covenanted together concerning the kingdom. Jonathan was the leader of a conspiracy that included some of the very men Saul was addressing. These traitors were working for David because David had promised to reward them. Furthermore, Saul was sure that David was plotting to kill him!

Doeg told the truth when he said he saw David at Nob and that Ahimelech the high priest gave him food and the sword of Goliath. But there's no evidence that the high priest used the Urim and Thummim to determine the will of God for David (Ex. 28:30; Num. 27:21). The sword of Goliath was kept near the ephod, and Ahimelech may have seen the high priest with the ephod in his hand, but this wasn't evidence that Ahimelech had consulted God on behalf of David. However, the lie made Doeg look good and David look bad.

The illegal trial (1 Sam. 22:11-15). It was but a short distance from Gibeah to Nob, so Saul immediately sent for the high priest, all his family, and the priests of Nob. Saul refused to address the high priest by his given name, but like Doeg called him "the son of Ahitub." The name Ahimelech means "brother of the king" and Saul wanted nothing to do with that, while "Ahitub" means "good brother." The king was obviously doing all he could to disgrace the high priest, when he should have been confessing his sins and seeking God's forgiveness. Saul was actually conducting an illegal trial, presenting four charges: Ahimelech gave David bread, he provided him with a weapon, he inquired of God for him, and he therefore was part of David's "conspiracy" to kill Saul so that he could become king. Never was Saul's paranoia more evident or more dangerous.

When Ahimelech heard these accusations, he first defended David before giving an account of his own actions. He reminded the king that David had been a faithful servant, an argument Saul's own son Jonathan had previously used (19:4-5). The entire nation honored David as a courageous and faithful warrior. But even more, David was Saul's son-in-law, a member of the royal family, one who had always done the king's bidding. He was held in high esteem in the king's household and even served as captain of Saul's personal bodyguard (22:14, NIV). If he had wanted to kill Saul, David certainly had plenty of opportunities to do so even before he fled. Perhaps the priest's words reminded the king that it was Saul who tried to kill David, not David who tried to kill Saul.

Ahimelech denied using the ephod to determine God's will for David. In fact, he stated boldly that if he had done so, it would have been the first time, because he had never done so before.[11] To do so would have been to forsake Saul for David! He closed his defense by stating that he and his family knew nothing about any conspiracy and therefore could in no way take part in a conspiracy.

The unjust sentence (1 Sam. 22:16-19). There was no evidence that Ahimelech had ever committed a capital crime, but Saul announced that he and his household must die. Even if the high priest had been guilty, which he was not, it was illegal to punish the whole family for the father's crime (Deut. 24:16). Their crime was knowing that David had fled and not reporting it to Saul. The things that Samuel had warned about the monarchy *and even more* were now taking place (1 Sam. 8:10-18). Saul had a police state in which each citizen was to spy on the others and report to the king anybody who opposed his rule. Israel had asked for a king "like the other nations," and that's what they received!

The guards nearest the king ("footmen," KJV) refused to slay the priests. (This reminds us of the time Saul commanded the people to kill Jonathan for violating the oath, and they refused to obey him

(14:41-46). Saul knew that Doeg was ready to do the evil deed, so he gave him permission to execute Ahimelech and his household, eighty-five priests of the Lord. A liar and murderer at heart (John 8:44), Doeg went beyond Saul's orders and went to Nob where he wiped out the entire population as well as the farm animals.

While this unjust trial and illegal sentence disturbs us, we must keep in mind that it was part of God's plan. This slaughter of the priests was a partial fulfillment of the ominous prophecy that had been given to unfaithful Eli (1 Sam. 2:27-36; 4:10-18), for God promised to replace the house of Eli with the house of Zadok (1 Kings 2:26-27; 4:2).

The protected priest (1 Sam. 22:20-23). The only survivor of the massacre at Nob was Abiathar, a son of Ahimelech, who then became the high priest. He knew that his only hope was to join David, so he fled to Keilah where David was now camped (23:6). When David moved from Hereth to Keilah isn't revealed in the text, but having a priest with an ephod was a tremendous help to David and his company. The 400 men had Gad the prophet, Abiathar the priest, and David the king; and they were fighting the battles of the Lord.[12] David took the blame for the slaughter of the priests, but he also took the responsibility of caring for Abiathar and making sure he was safe.

David was now officially an outlaw, but the Lord was with him and he would one day become Israel's greatest king.

NINE

David the Deliverer

In the second chapter of his book *Up from Slavery*, Booker T. Washington wrote, "I have learned that success is to be measured not so much by the position that one has reached in life as by the obstacles which he has overcome while trying to succeed." Measured by this standard—and it's a valid one—David was a very successful man. For ten years he was considered an outlaw, yet he fought the Lord's battles and delivered Israel from her enemies. He lived with his faithful men in the forsaken places of the land and often had to flee for his life, yet he knew that the Lord would finally deliver him and give him the promised throne. David's coronation was not only important to the people of Israel; it was important to all the people of God of every age. For out of David's family the Redeemer would ultimately come, Jesus of Nazareth, the Son of David, the Son of God.

1. David delivers Keilah from the Philistines (1 Sam. 23:1–6)
Keilah was a border town in Judah, about twelve miles from the Philistine city of Gath and some ten miles west of the forest of Hereth where David and his men were camping (22:5). Situated that close to the enemy, Keilah was extremely vulnerable, especially during the

harvest season when the Philistine army was searching for food. Had King Saul been concerned about defending his people instead, he would have sent a detachment of soldiers to protect Keilah, but he was obsessed with finding David and killing him.

The spies of both David and Saul were active in the land, and David's spies reported that the Philistines were attacking Keilah. David paused to determine the will of God, a practice every leader needs to imitate, for it's easy for our own personal interests to get in the way of God's will. How did David discover God's will when Abiathar the priest hadn't yet arrived in the camp? (23:6) The prophet Gad was with David (22:5), and it's likely that he prayed to the Lord for direction. Once Abiathar arrived with the ephod, David had him inquire of the Lord when there were important decisions to make (v. 9; 25:32; 26:11, 23).[1]

Once David got the go-ahead signal from the Lord, he mobilized his men, but they weren't too enthusiastic about his plans. It was acceptable to fight the Philistines, Israel's long-time enemies, but they didn't want to fight their own Jewish brothers. What if Saul turned against David and his men? The band of 600 men would then be caught between two armies! Unwilling to impose his own ideas on his men, David sought the Lord's will a second time, and once again he was told to go rescue the people of Keilah. It wasn't David's unbelief that created the problem, because he had faith in the Lord, but the fear in the hearts of his men made them unprepared for battle.

God more than kept His promise because He not only helped David slaughter the invading Philistines but also take a great amount of spoil from them. David moved into Keilah, which was a walled city, and it was there that Abiathar went when he fled from Nob carrying the precious ephod (22:20-23; 23:6). But Saul's spies were at work and learned that David was now in Keilah, a walled city with gates. Saul told his troops they were going to Keilah to rescue the city, but his real purpose was to capture David, and he was certain that David could not escape. Saul was not only willing to slaughter the priests of Nob, but he would have destroyed his own people in the city of Keilah just to lay hands on David. People who are controlled by malice and hatred quickly lose their perspective and begin to abuse their authority.

2. David delivers himself and his men from Saul (1 Sam. 23:7-29)
While serving on Saul's staff, David had dodged the king's spears, thwarted an attempted kidnapping, and escaped the intended violence of three companies of soldiers and of Saul himself. Now that he was a fugitive with a price on his head and had over six hundred people to care for, David had to be very careful what he did and where he went. There might be another Doeg hiding in the shadows.

From Keilah to the wilderness of Ziph (1 Sam. 23:7-18). David's spies quickly let him know that Saul was planning to come to Keilah, so with Abiathar's help, David sought the Lord's guidance. His great concern was whether the people of Keilah would turn him and his men over to Saul. Since David had rescued the city from the Philistines, you would have expected the citizens to be grateful and to protect David, but such was not the case.[2] The Lord warned David to get out of the city because the people were prepared to turn him over to the king. No doubt the people of Keilah were afraid that if they didn't cooperate with Saul, he would massacre them as he did the people in Nob. David recalled how pained he was because of the tragedy at Nob, and he didn't want another city wiped out because of him. He led his men out and they "kept moving from place to place" (v. 13, NIV) until they settled in the wilderness of Ziph (v. 14).

When Saul got the word that David had left Keilah, he called off the attack, but he still sought him day after day and neglected the important affairs of the kingdom. However, the Lord was on David's side and made sure that Saul was never successful in his quest. Ziph was a town fifteen miles southeast of Keilah in "the wilderness of Ziph" which was part of "the wilderness of Judah." This is a destitute area adjacent to the Dead Sea where David's faith and courage were greatly tested. When visitors to the Holy Land see this wilderness area, they often express amazement that David could ever survive living there.

David's beloved friend Jonathan risked his life to visit David in the wilderness and "helped him find strength in God" (v. 16, NIV). This was their last recorded meeting. Jonathan isn't mentioned again in 1 Samuel until 31:2 where we're told he died on the battlefield. Jonathan had no idea that he would be slain before David became king, because he talked with David about their future coregency and renewed with him the covenant they had made (18:8; 20:31). He assured David that God would surely make him king in His good time, and that David would always be delivered from Saul's schemes to capture him. Jonathan admitted that his father knew all these plans.

From Ziph to the wilderness of Maon (1 Sam. 23:19-28). The Ziphites weren't interested in following God's plan; their great concern was to protect themselves from the rage of King Saul. They knew where David was hiding so they conveyed this important information to Saul, carefully addressing him as "king." This was their way of assuring him that they were loyal to him and not to David. Saul was still manipulating people by making them feel sorry for him (v. 21; 22:8), and this combination of building personal pity and wielding ruthless power seemed to be working. But Saul's character was deteriorating very quickly, while the Lord was molding David into a courageous man of God.

Saul was a good enough warrior to know that he couldn't find David in the wilderness of Judah without some specific directions, so he asked the Ziphites to send him exact details. He wanted to know the hiding places in the rocks and caves that David frequented and the hidden paths that he took. Once he had the map, Saul could search out the area and quickly find his enemy. But David also had his spies working and knew what Saul was doing, and the Lord was watching over the future king. David moved out of the area of Ziph and three miles south into the wilderness of Maon.

But Saul wasn't about to give up, so he followed David into the wilderness of Maon, and the two armies met at "the rock," a well-known mountain in the area. Saul divided his army and sent half around one side of the mountain and half around the other side, a pincers movement that would have meant total defeat for David and his 600 soldiers. But the Lord was in control and brought the Philistines to attack somewhere in Judah, and Saul and his men had to abandon the attack. It was a close call for David, but God kept His promises. To commemorate this great escape, the Jews called the place "Sela Hammahlekoth," which means "the rock of parting." The Hebrew carries the idea of "a smooth rock" and therefore "a slippery rock," in other words, "the rock of slipping away." David quickly moved from Maon to Engedi, next to the Dead Sea, a place of safety with an ample water supply.

David wrote Psalm 54 on this occasion and in it prayed for salvation and vindication from the Lord. David knew that the flatterers in Saul's official circle, people like Doeg, were telling lies about him and making it look as though David wanted to kill the king. These fawning toadies were hoping to be rewarded by Saul, but they only went down in defeat because they gave allegiance to the wrong king. Leaders who enjoy flattery and praise, and who encourage and reward associates who seek only to gratify their leader's ego, can never build other leaders or accomplish the will of God to the glory of God. David developed officers who were "mighty men" (1 Chron. 21; 2 Sam. 24), but Saul attracted officers who were moral weaklings. "Therefore by their fruits you will know them" (Matt. 7:20).

3. David delivers Saul from death (1 Sam. 24:1-22)

David had prayed in Psalm 54 that the Lord would vindicate him and give him opportunity to prove to Saul that he wasn't an outlaw who was trying to kill him and seize the throne. After all, Saul was not only David's king, but he was also his commander and his father-in-law, and regardless of Saul's evil attitude, David never considered Saul to be his enemy.[3] God answered David's prayer when Saul and his troops came to find him at Engedi.

David's temptation (1 Sam. 24: 1-4). David and his men were hiding in a large cave, of which there were many in that area, and Saul chose to use that very cave as a place where he could relieve himself. The Law of Moses was very strict when it came to matters of sanitation, especially in the army camp (Deut. 23:12-14). Each soldier was required to leave the camp to relieve himself, and he had to carry a small shovel or trowel among his weapons so he could dig a hole and cover his excrement. This meant that Saul was away from the camp and therefore quite vulnerable. He naturally wanted privacy and he felt that he was not in danger. The fact that he walked right into David's hiding place not only proved that his spies were incompetent but also that the Lord was still in control.

As David and his men pressed to the walls in the back of the cave, they quietly discussed the meaning of this remarkable occurrence. The men assured David that Saul's presence in the cave was the fulfillment of a promise God gave him that He would deliver Saul into David's hands.[4] But when did God say this? Were they referring to Samuel's words to Saul in 1 Samuel 15:26-29, or to God's message to Samuel in 16:1? Perhaps the idea came from Jonathan's words in 20:15, which some of the men might have heard personally. It's likely that the leaders of the 600 men discussed these matters among themselves, for their future was wrapped up in David's future, and obviously they came to some false conclusions. David never planned to kill Saul, for he was sure that the Lord would remove him from the scene in His own way and His own time (26:9-11).

To David's men, it seemed providential that Saul was at their mercy (24:4; Ex. 21:13), and both David and Saul agreed with them (1 Sam. 24:10, 18). But that wasn't the issue. The major question was, "How does the Lord want us to use this occasion?" David's men saw it as an opportunity for revenge, while David saw it as an opportunity to show mercy and prove that his heart was right. God was giving him an opportunity to answer his own prayer for vindication (Ps. 54:1). David stealthily crept up to the garment that Saul had laid aside, cut off a corner of the robe, and went back into the cave. Saul left the cave not realizing what had happened.

David's conviction (1 Sam. 24:5-7) David was too wise in the truth of God's word to interpret this event as a signal for him to kill Saul, for the law says, "You shall not murder" (Ex. 20:13, NIV). Slaying an enemy on the battlefield or an attacker in self-defense was one thing, but to assassinate an unsuspecting king was quite something else. David reminded his men that Saul was the anointed of the Lord, and that no Jew had the right to attack him. The Jews were not even to curse their rulers, let alone kill them, for cursing a ruler was in the same category as blaspheming the name of the Lord (22:28).

However, David's conscience bothered him because he had cut off the corner of Saul's robe. His action sent out three messages. First, it was an insolent act of disrespect that humiliated Saul, but it was also a symbolic gesture not unlike what Saul did to Samuel's robe after the Amalekite fiasco (1 Sam. 15:27-28). By cutting off a part of the royal robe, David was declaring that the kingdom had been transferred to him. Finally, the piece of cloth was proof that David did not intend to kill the king and that the flatterers in the court were all liars. David's men would have killed Saul in a moment, but their wise captain restrained them. Leaders must know how to interpret events and respond in the right way.

David's vindication (1 Sam. 24: 8-15). When Saul was far enough away from the cave that it was safe, David left the cave and called to him. By using the title "my lord the king" and bowing to the earth, David emphasized what he had said to his men and let Saul know that he was not a rebel. Even if you can't respect the man or woman in office, you must show respect to the office (Rom. 13:1-7; 1 Peter 2:13-17). David showed his respect by calling Saul "my master" (1 Sam. 24:6), "the Lord's anointed" (vv. 6, 10), "my lord" (vv. 8, 10), "the king" (vv. 8, 14) and "my father" (v. 14). David's bold public appearance also let Saul and his army know that their official spy system was most ineffective.

Using the piece of Saul's robe as evidence, David opened his defense by exposing the deception of the courtiers who slandered David to Saul. The logic was irrefutable: David had an opportunity to kill Saul and refused to do so. David even admitted that some of his men urged him to slay the king, but he rebuked them. David was not guilty of any evil against Saul or any transgression against the Lord, but Saul was guilty of trying to kill David. "The Lord will judge between us," said David, "and prove that your officers are liars, but I will not lift my hand against you." Saul had hoped that the hand of the Philistines (18:17) or the hands of David's soldiers (19:20-21) would kill David, but they failed. Ultimately, Saul died by his own hand on the battlefield (31:1-6).

David quoted a familiar proverb[5] to prove his point: "Wickedness proceeds from the wicked" (24:13, NKJV), which simply means that character is revealed by conduct. The fact that David did not slay the king indicated that David did not have the character of a rebel or a murderer. But at the same time, David was strongly suggesting that Saul's character was questionable because he wanted to kill his son-in-law! But what was the king really doing as he pursued David? Only chasing a dead dog and a flea that was jumping from one place to another! (Fleas and dogs go together.) The phrase "dead dog" was a humiliating term of reproach in those days (17:43; 2 Sam. 3:8; 9:8; 16:9), so David was humbling himself before the Lord and the king. David closed his defense by asserting a second time (1 Sam. 24:12, 15) that the Lord was the righteous judge and would plead the cause of His faithful servant (Pss. 35:1; 43:1; see 1 Peter 2:23).

David's affirmation (1 Sam. 24:16-22). King Saul once again revealed his confused mental state by lifting up his voice and calling to David, who had certainly spoken long enough for Saul to discern that it was indeed his son-in-law.[6] As for Saul's weeping, he had manifested temporary emotional reactions like that before, but they never brought about repentance or a change of heart.

Saul described three possible levels of life: the divine level, where we return good for evil; the human level, where we return good for good and evil for evil; and the demonic level, where we return evil for good. Saul admitted that David was a godly man who, by not slaying him, returned good for evil. But Saul was possessed by demonic forces and did evil to the one man who could have destroyed him. Now Saul openly confessed that he knew David would be the next king (23:17) and would consolidate the nation of Israel that Saul had torn apart. Even then, Saul's major concern was his own name and descendants, not the spiritual welfare of the people; he made David swear that he wouldn't wipe out his family when he became king. David had made a similar covenant with Jonathan (20:14-17, 42) and he was willing to make the same promise to Saul. How tragic that Saul's own sins destroyed his family, all but Jonathan's crippled son, Mephibosheth, whom David adopted (2 Sam. 9).

Because David knew God's calling and believed God's promise, he was able to be so bold before Saul and his army. It was indeed a holy boldness that came from a heart that was right with God. The day would come when David and his cause would be vindicated and the Lord would judge those who had opposed him. Saul went back home to Gibeah, but in spite of his tears and emotional speech, he took up his pursuit of David again (1 Sam. 26:2, 21).

David had won many battles, but one of his greatest victories occurred in that cave when he restrained himself and his men from killing Saul. "He who is slow to anger is better than the mighty, and he who rules his spirit than he who takes a city" (Prov. 16:32, NKJV). This is a good example for all of us to follow, but especially those to whom the Lord has entrusted leadership.

TEN

1 SAMUEL 25–26

A Wise Woman and a Foolish King

Personal relationships are a large part of our lives, the most important being our relationship to the Lord. If from childhood you and I had kept a list of all the significant people who came in and out of our lives, we'd be amazed at their number and the variety of roles they played. Leaving God out of the picture, the longshoreman philosopher Eric Hoffer said that other people were "the playwrights and stage managers of our lives: they cast us in a role and we play it whether we will or no." But you can't leave God out of the picture! After all, He's the one who writes the script for us, chooses the cast, and puts us into the scenes He's planned for us. If we follow His directions, life becomes the satisfying fulfillment of His will, but if we rebel, the plot turns into tragedy.

These two chapters record four events that reveal David's involvement with four different kinds of people.

1. David loses a friend (1 Sam. 25:1)

The death of Samuel, Israel's prophet and judge, is mentioned twice in the book (28:3). Both references state that all Israel mourned his death and gathered to bury him. Of course, not every Israelite attended the funeral service, but the leaders of the tribes were present to pay their last respects to a great man. It was Samuel's faith and courage that helped the nation transition from political disunity to a somewhat united monarchy. Since Saul and Samuel had been alienated for over seven years, it's not likely that the king attended the funeral, but he would call on Samuel for help even after the prophet was dead (chap. 28).

The people of Israel didn't always obey Samuel when he was alive, but they were careful to honor him when he died. Such is human nature (Matt. 23:29-31). However, Samuel didn't prepare an elaborate tomb for himself at some important public place, but instead asked to be buried at his own house in Ramah, probably in the garden or in a courtyard. In his pride, King Saul had prepared a public monument to himself at Carmel (1 Sam. 15:12), but Samuel, who truly deserved recognition, humbly asked to be laid to rest at his own home.

David knew it would be dangerous for him to attend the funeral at Ramah, for Saul would have his spies there, so he retreated to the wilderness. David had shown his love and respect for Samuel while the prophet was alive, so there was no need for him to make a public appearance. Samuel had anointed David king of Israel and had often protected David and given him counsel. How wonderful it is when the saints of the older generation spend time with the younger leaders and help to prepare them to serve the Lord and His people, and how encouraging it is when the younger leaders listen and learn.

Samuel was the kind of spiritual mentor and counselor that every leader needs, because he put the concerns of God ahead of the politics of the hour. To Samuel, pleasing the Lord was far more important than being popular with the people. It broke his heart when Israel asked for a king, but he obeyed the Lord's orders and anointed Saul. It wasn't long before he was disappointed in Saul, but then the Lord led him to anoint David. Samuel died knowing that the kingdom would be in good hands.

David was in Masada ("the stronghold") when Samuel died (24:22), and he and his men left there for the "wilderness of

Paran," more than a hundred miles south of Masada. Perhaps David felt that the loss of Samuel's influence and prayers meant greater danger for him and therefore he needed more distance between himself and Saul. Instead of "Paran," some texts read "Maon," a place of refuge near the Dead Sea where David had been before (23:24). The events in the story of Nabal occur in Maon near Carmel (25:2), and this suggests that Maon may have been David's hiding place. Perhaps David fled to Paran and then backtracked to Maon, but considering the nature of the terrain and the difficulty of travel, this idea seems untenable.

David discovers an enemy (1 Sam. 25:2-13)

During David's previous stay in the wilderness of Maon (23:24ff), which is in the vicinity of Carmel,[1] his men had been a wall of protection for Nabal's flocks and those caring for them. Nabal was a very wealthy man, but he was not a generous man. When David returned to Nabal's neighborhood, it was shearing time, a festive event (2 Sam. 13:23) that occurred each spring and early fall. David hoped that Nabal would reward him and his men for their service, for certainly they deserved something for protecting Nabal's sheep and goats from the thieves that usually showed up at shearing time.

David's expectation was logical. Any man with 3,000 sheep and 1,000 goats could easily spare a few animals to feed 600 men who had risked their own lives to guard part of his wealth. Common courtesy would certainly dictate that Nabal invite David and his men to share his food at a festive season when hospitality was the order of the day. It wouldn't be easy to feed 600 men in the wilderness, so David sent ten of his young men to explain the situation and to ask to be invited to the feast. Nabal refused to listen.

The character of Nabal is described as "churlish and evil" (1 Sam. 25:3), which the NIV translates "surly and mean" and the NLT "mean and dishonest in all his dealings." (Did he become rich by being dishonest?) He was from the tribe of Judah and the family of Caleb, one of the two spies who urged Israel to enter the

Promised Land (Num. 13-14; Josh. 14:6-7).[2] But the name "Caleb" also means "a dog," so perhaps the writer was conveying this meaning as well. The man was like a stubborn vicious animal that nobody could safely approach (1 Sam. 25:17). One of his own servants *and his own wife* both called him "a son of Belial—a worthless fellow" (vv. 17, 25). The Hebrew word *beliya'al* means "worthlessness" and in the Old Testament refers to evil people who deliberately broke the law and despised what was good. (See Deut. 13:13; Jud. 19:22; 20:13; 1 Sam. 2:12.) In the New Testament, the word refers also to Satan (2 Cor. 6:15).

When the young men graciously presented their case, Nabal "railed on them," which the NIV translates "hurled insults at them." The Hebrew word describes the shrieking of a bird of prey as it swoops down to tear its victim. It's used to describe Saul's hungry men as they fell on the plunder and butchered the animals (1 Sam. 14:32; 15:19). His words are found in 25:10-11 and certainly reveal the heart of a man who is selfish, arrogant, and rebellious. Abigail recognized David as king (vv. 28 and 30) and called David "my lord," but Nabal compared David to a rebellious servant who abandoned his master! (v. 10) It's obvious that Nabal's sympathies lay with Saul and not with David, another evidence that he had no heart for spiritual matters as his wife did. When you note all the personal pronouns in verse 11, you immediately recognize his pride and self-importance. He didn't even give God credit for making him wealthy! (Deut. 8:17-18; Luke 12:15-21)

The young men reported Nabal's reply to David who immediately became angry and swore revenge on him. David could forgive Saul, who wanted to kill him, but he couldn't forgive Nabal who only refused to feed him and his men. Nabal was ungrateful and selfish, but those are not capital crimes; Saul was envious and consumed with the desire to kill an innocent man. David's anger got the best of him; he didn't stop to consult the Lord, and he rushed out to satisfy his passion for revenge. Had David succeeded, he would have committed a terrible sin and done great damage to his character and his career, but the Lord mercifully stopped him.

God's servants need to be on guard at all times lest the enemy suddenly attack and conquer them. "Be sober, be vigilant, because your adversary the devil walks about like a roaring lion, seeking whom he may devour" (1 Peter 5:8, NKJV). David was a godly man and a gifted leader, but the best of men are but men at their best.

3. David takes a wife (1 Sam. 25:14-44)

When the Lord isn't allowed to rule in our lives, then He steps in and overrules. He saw that David was about to act rashly and foolishly, so He arranged for a wise and courageous woman to stop him.

Abigail's wise plan (1 Sam. 25:14-19). When this anonymous young man reported his master's actions to Abigail, he was serving the Lord whether he knew it or not. He knew he couldn't talk to Nabal about anything (v. 17), so he immediately went to his mistress, a wise and prudent woman. In those days, the parents arranged marriages for their children, so we aren't surprised to see a wise woman married to a foolish man. (Alas, it often happens today without the help of parents!) No doubt Abigail's parents considered it fortunate that their daughter could marry such a wealthy man, and she obeyed their wishes, but her life with Nabal must have been tedious. All her husband was interested in was money, food and drink, and having his own way.

The servant reported how David and his men had protected the shepherds and their flocks, and how Nabal had refused to repay them. Did the young man know that David and his men were on their way to confront Nabal, or did he simply surmise it? Perhaps it was the Lord who gave him a special intuition that trouble was coming. Nabal and his servants were defenseless against David's 400 men. But if David had succeeded in this venture, it would have given Saul the evidence he needed that David was a dangerous renegade who had to be dealt with drastically.

Abigail put together enough food for David's men but said nothing to her husband. She was the mistress of the house and could dispose of the family provisions as she saw fit, even to the extent of sharing it with others. Nabal would have opposed her even though she was doing it for his own good. She wasn't stealing from her husband; she was paying a debt that he refused to pay. In order to save a little money, Nabal was foolishly jeopardizing the lives of everybody in his household, especially his own.

Abigail's humble apology (1 Sam. 25:20-35). Only a sovereign Lord could have arranged the timing of David's attack and Abigail's approach so that the two bands met. Abigail bowed before David and acknowledged him as her lord and king; in fact, she used the word "lord" fourteen times in her speech. Nabal would not have approved of her words or her actions because he was a follower of Saul and considered David a rebel (v. 10). Abigail was a woman of faith who believed that David was God's king, and she saw King Saul as only "a man" (v. 29). She quickly confessed that her husband was a "worthless fellow" (v. 25, see v. 17) who lived up to his name—fool, and she explained that she had known nothing about David's request for food. She accepted the blame for "this iniquity" (vv. 24, 28).[3]

In the rest of her speech, Abigail focused on David and the Lord and not on David and Nabal, and her emphasis was on David's future. By now David was calming down and starting to realize that he was in the presence of a remarkable woman. She pointed out that the Lord had stopped David from avenging himself, and David admitted this was true (vv. 32-34). Abigail admitted that her husband deserved to be judged, but she wanted the Lord to do it, not the king. In fact, she promised that the Lord would judge *all* the enemies of the king.

Abigail reminded David that the Lord had given him "a sure house" ("lasting dynasty," NIV), so he didn't have to fear the future. David was safe, bound in "the bundle of life" by the Lord; but his enemies would be hurled out like the stone David used when he defeated Goliath (see Jer. 10:18). No matter what Saul planned to do to David, the Lord would keep His promises and make David ruler over Israel. Then David would be glad he hadn't shed blood in order to avenge himself or get to the throne. The Lord would treat David well and he had nothing to fear.

Abigail had only one request for herself: that David would remember her when he came into his kingdom (1 Sam. 25:31). Was this a veiled suggestion of marriage, should Nabal die? Or was Abigail merely looking ahead and seeing herself as a widow who could profit from friendship with the king? Perhaps she was cautioning David to remember her and her advice when he became king so he wouldn't be tempted to take things into his own hands and forget the will of the Lord. As it turned out, David didn't wait too long after Nabal's decease but took her as his wife!

David blessed the Lord for providentially stopping him from killing innocent people, and he also blessed Abigail for her wise advice. David was a smart man to listen to reproof wisely given (Prov. 15:5, 10, 31-33); it's not likely that Saul would have listened to a woman's counsel. David wrote in Psalm 141:5, "Let the righteous strike me; it shall be a kindness. And let him reprove me; it shall be as excellent oil; let my head not refuse it" (NKJV). How we receive reproof and counsel is a test of our relationship to the Lord and our willingness to live by His Word. David admitted that he was wrong, the Lord forgave him, and the Lord worked out the problem for him.

Abigail's unexpected marriage (1 Sam. 25:36-44). Nabal is feasting when judgment is just around the corner! He didn't stop to thank God for the blessings He had sent to him, or even to consider that these blessings came because of his wife's faith and in spite of his own meanness. Nabal's idea of happiness wasn't to praise God or feed the hungry, but to eat to the full and get drunk. Nabal made no profession of faith in the Lord but was like the people Paul described: "whose end is destruction, whose god is their belly, and whose glory is in their shame—who set their mind on earthly things" (Phil. 3:19, NKJV).

Wisely, Abigail waited to tell her husband what she had done. The news so stunned Nabal that he experienced a stroke and lay helpless for ten days, and then the Lord took his life. What caused the stroke? Was it pride and anger on learning that his wife had dared to help David without his permission? Or was it shock in realizing the danger he had been in and how close he and his household had come to being slain? What if Saul heard that Abigail had befriended David? The king might consider Nabal an enemy and punish him accordingly. Whether one or all of these considerations caused Nabal's paralysis, it was the Lord who ultimately took his life. Sad to say, he died as he had lived—a fool.

When David heard the news of Nabal's death, he praised the Lord for avenging him and preventing him from doing it himself. David's concern was the glory of God and the advancement of His kingdom. Abigail certainly must have been pleased to be set free from the yoke of such a wicked man, a man she probably married against her will. David had been so impressed with her character and wisdom that he thought she would make a good queen, so he sent messengers to ask for her hand in marriage. It was an opportunity no woman would refuse, and she submitted to her king and even offered to wash his feet! In marrying Abigail, David not only acquired a good wife, but he also got possession of all of Nabal's wealth and property, which was situated near Hebron where David later established his royal residence (2 Sam. 2:1-4; 5:5). He had already taken Ahinoam as his wife, since she is always named before Abigail (27:3; 30:5; 2 Sam. 2:2). She was the mother of David's firstborn son, Amnon, and Abigail bore him Kileab, also named Daniel (1 Chron. 3:2).

But what about David's first wife, Michal, Saul's daughter, who had helped to save David's life? After David fled from home, Saul gave her to another man, probably using the alliance as a means to strengthen his own position and to break David's connection with the throne. There was no legal divorce, so Saul forced Michal into an adulterous relationship. When David was reigning over the tribe of Judah in Hebron, he demanded that Michal be returned to him (2 Sam. 3:13-16). However, Michal didn't remain a loving wife and probably resented David's taking her father's throne. She died childless (6:16-23).

4. David spares the king (1 Sam. 26:1-15)
Some students of the Old Testament have tried to prove that the account in this chapter is merely an adaptation of the one in

chapter 24, but the evidence stands against this interpretation. There are differences in locations (a cave in En Gedi; Saul's camp near Hachilah), times (day; night), activities (Saul came to the cave; David went to the camp), David's responses (cutting off part of Saul's robe; taking Saul's spear and water jug), and David's words (spoke only to Saul; spoke to Abner and Saul). This second experience with Saul was certainly more daring on David's part since he was actually in Saul's camp. David's recent experience with Nabal and Abigail had reassured him of his future reign and had taught him a profitable lesson about revenge.

Treachery (1 Sam. 26:1-4). Like Nabal, the Ziphites were related to Caleb (1 Chron. 2:42), but being members of the tribe of Judah, they should have been loyal to David. Hoping to gain the king's approval, for a second time they betrayed David to Saul (1 Sam. 23:19ff; see Ps. 54). Saul had learned to appreciate David's skill as a tactician, so he took his 3,000 soldiers to search for David in the wilderness. But David was already far ahead of him, for his spies had located Saul's camp, and David was safe in the desert. The Lord kept David safe and delivered him whenever Saul was near. "He delivered me from my strong enemy, from those who hated me, for they were too strong for me" (Ps. 18:17, NKJV).

Audacity (1 Sam. 26: 5-12). The Lord must have instructed David to go to Saul's camp that night, because He sent a deep sleep upon Saul and his men. Saul and Abner, who was Saul's captain (14:10) and cousin (v. 50), were sleeping at the heart of the camp, surrounded by the wagons and baggage ("the trench" KJV). Because of the supernatural sleep sent by the Lord, David and his nephew Abishai were able to penetrate to where Saul and Abner lay.[4] This is the first mention of Abishai in Scripture. As usual, Saul's spear was at hand, the symbol of his office and his authority (26:7, 11; 22:6; 18:10; 19:9; 20:33).

Abishai was sure that it was God's will that he kill Saul and put an end to his selfish rule and his relentless persecution of Israel's true king, but David stopped him. David had settled this matter in the cave (24:1-6) and there was no need to consider it again. He had also seen what the Lord did to Nabal. David was sure that Saul's life would end at the right time and in the right way, either by natural death or by a judgment from God, and then the throne would be his. When Abishai looked at Saul, he saw an enemy, but David looked at him and saw "the Lord's anointed." Instead of taking Saul's life, David took his spear and water jug, just so he could prove to Saul a second time that he didn't have designs on the king's life. David didn't let Abishai take the spear lest he be tempted to use it.

It would have been easy to argue that David had been wrong in the cave and that God was giving him a second chance to kill Saul, but David's decision was based on principle and not circumstances. David knew that it was wrong to lay hands on God's anointed, even though the king wasn't serving as God wanted him to serve. David might not have been able to respect the man, but he did respect the office and the God who gave that office to Saul.

Mockery (1 Sam. 26:13-16). David and his nephew made their way to the hill opposite Saul's camp where they were safe and from which they could be heard, and David called back to the soldiers in the camp and especially to Abner, the king's bodyguard. He was careful not to humiliate Saul in the presence of his men, although Saul couldn't easily escape the embarrassment of the situation. David didn't identify himself to Abner but only referred to himself as "one of the people" (v. 15). The absence of the spear and water jug was evidence enough that someone indeed had been close to the king and could have killed him. Abner was guilty and could have been disciplined for not doing his duty.

Dishonesty (vv. 17-25). Saul recognized David's voice and responded by calling him "my son, David", but David didn't call him "my father" as he had before (24:11). His address was only "my lord, O king." Saul's daughter Michal was no longer David's wife (25:44), so David was no longer son-in-law to the king. Furthermore, Saul certainly hadn't treated David like a son.

Once again, David tried to reason with Saul and show him

how wrong he was in his thinking and acting. David wanted to know what his crime was that Saul had to pursue him and seek to kill him. If David had broken one of God's laws, then he was willing to bring a sacrifice and have his sin forgiven by the Lord. But if Saul was treating David like a criminal because of the lies his officers had told him, then *they* were the offenders, not David, and they would pay for their sins. Saul and his officers had driven David out of his own land, the very inheritance that the Lord had given his family, and if David moved to other lands, how could he worship Jehovah away from the priesthood and the sanctuary?[5]

But if David wasn't guilty of any crime or sin, why should Saul invest so much time and energy in pursuing him? The king of Israel was chasing a partridge just for the privilege of shedding its blood! (Partridges don't like to fly. They run from one cover to another.)

Once again, Saul lapsed into one of his sentimental moods (see 24:17) and confessed that he was a fool and a sinner. He promised that he wouldn't harm David, but David didn't believe him. His only reply was, "Behold the king's spear! Let one of the young men come over and fetch it" (26:22). When David cut Saul's robe in the cave, he reminded him that his kingdom would be severed from him, but in taking the spear, he humiliated the king and robbed him of the symbol of his authority.

For the second time, David had spared Saul's life, and David knew that the Lord would reward him for what he had done (Ps. 7:8). But David didn't expect Saul to value his life as he had valued Saul's life, because he knew Saul couldn't be trusted. Rather, he asked that the Lord reward him with protection and safety just as he had protected the king. See Psalm 18:20-27.

The last recorded words of Saul to David are in 1 Samuel 26:25, a statement that affirms the greatness of David's deeds and the certainty of his kingship. The two men parted, Saul heading for ultimate disgrace and death, and David to ultimate glory and victory. However, David's unbelief would take him to the land of the Philistines and the city of Ziklag, where he would live for about a year and a half. Soon David's years of wandering and testing would end and he would be ready to sit on the throne of Israel and rule God's people. One day David would look back on those difficult years and see in his painful experiences only the goodness and mercy of the Lord (Ps. 23:6).

ELEVEN

1 SAMUEL 27:1–28;2; 29–30

Living with the Enemy

In his more mature years, David heard God say to him, "I will instruct you and teach you in the way you should go; I will guide you with My eye. Do not be like the horse or like the mule" (Ps. 32:8-9, NKJV). The horse is impulsive and rushes heedlessly into the battle, while the mule is stubborn and holds back; and all of us have had both experiences. God doesn't want to deal with us as men deal with animals; He wants to be close to us and guide us with His eye, the way a parent guides a child. When we behold the face of the Lord, we can see His smile or frown and we can discern from His eyes which way He wants us to go. These chapters record the experiences of David when he was living without that kind of intimate, loving guidance.

1. Departing from the land (1 Sam. 27:1-2)
David had been a fugitive for about seven years when he decided to flee to Gath, but the idea of leaving Israel had probably already been in his mind (26:19). David had every reason to stay in the land and continue to trust God for protection and provision. After all, he was the anointed king of Israel and knew that eventually God would give him the throne. Abigail assured him

of this (25:27-31), and even Saul admitted that David would ultimately triumph (26:25). Saul didn't keep one of his promises to leave David alone, and the constant flattery of the liars in his inner circle encouraged the king to keep on pursuing David. Living the life of a wilderness exile with his life daily in the balance was starting to depress David, and now he had two wives and 600 men to care for.

"How long, O Lord? Will you forget me forever? How long will you hide your face from me? How long shall I take counsel in my soul, having sorrow in my heart daily? How long will my enemy be exalted over me?" (Ps. 13:1-2, NKJV) In about three years, David's exile would end and he would be ruling the people of Judah in Hebron, but he had no way of knowing this. It takes both faith and patience to receive what God has promised (Heb. 6:12), and David seemed to be wavering in both of these essentials. He needed the faith and courage expressed in Psalm 27:1-3, but before we criticize him too severely, let's recall the time when we've done the same thing.

This scene reminds us of a similar situation in the life of our Lord as He faced the cross (John 12:20-33). "Now is my soul troubled, and what shall I say? 'Father, save me from this hour'? But for this purpose I came to this hour. Father, glorify your name" (12:27-28, NKJV). Jesus had the Father's glory uppermost in His heart, while David was concerned primarily for his own safety and comfort. Yet God was using the difficulties in David's life to make him a man of God and to prepare him for the throne, but now he decided to go his own way and solve his own problems.

God's children must be careful not to yield to despondency. Moses was discouraged over his heavy workload and wanted to die (Num. 11:15), and Elijah ran from the place of duty because of fear and discouragement (1 Kings 19). When we start to look at God through our circumstances instead of looking at our circumstances through God's eyes, we will lose faith, patience, and courage, and the enemy will triumph. "Trust in the Lord with all your heart, and lean not on your own understanding" (Prov. 3:5, NKJV).

"My times are in your hand; deliver me from the hand of my

enemies, and from those who persecute me" (Ps. 31:15).

2. Deceiving the enemy (1 Sam. 27:3–29:11)

At the beginning of his exile, David had fled to Gath for safety, only to discover that his life was still in danger, and then he had to act like a madman in order to escape (21:10-15). But at that time, David was alone, while now he had two wives and was the commander of 600 valiant soldiers. David was still a deceiver, and "faith is living without scheming." He deceived Achish concerning three matters: the request for a city, the raids his men conducted, and the desire to fight the king's battles.

His request for a city (1 Sam. 27:3-7). Undoubtedly the news had reached the Philistines that Saul was trying to kill David, and so any enemy of Saul would be warmly welcomed in Gath. Achish could make use of David's tactical skill and the battle-honed skills of his courageous men. But the total number of people David brought with him could well have been between 2,000–3,000 (30:1-3), and that was quite a crowd to drop into the city of Gath.

Actually, David didn't want to stay in Gath because there the king and his officers could investigate what he was doing, so he requested that the king give him and his people a city of their own. He was very diplomatic in the way he phrased his request, humbling himself before the king ("I am not worthy to live in the royal city.") and assuring Achish that his services were always available. Happy to get the extra people out of Gath, where they were probably straining the food and water supply, and ready to strengthen his own army, Achish quickly accepted the idea. He gave David Ziklag, a town about twenty-five miles southwest of Gath, on the border of Simeon but under Philistine control. The tribe of Simeon had its inheritance within the tribe of Judah, which explains why Ziklag was associated with both tribes (Josh. 15:31; 19:5). However, since Achish gave the town to David, it belonged to the kings of Judah ever after. There could not have been a better base of operations for David and his men, and they made good use of it.

His reports of the raids (1 Sam. 27:8-12). Achish thought that David and his band were attacking cities and towns in Judah, when in reality they were raiding the towns and camps of the allies of Achish! David was wiping out the people that Joshua and his successors failed to exterminate when they entered the land, following the orders given by Moses in Deuteronomy 20:16-18. At the same time, he was eliminating the danger of any survivors taking the word to Gath that David was a liar. David took Achish gifts from the spoils of battle and gave him false reports of their activities, and Achish believed him. When word got back to the people of Judah that David was attacking their enemies, this made him even more popular with the leaders.

His responsibility in the battle (1 Sam. 28:1-2; 29:1-11). This is the battle in which Saul and his sons were killed (31:1-6), and it was the providential hand of the Lord that kept David and his men from having to participate. Achish assured David that he and his men were expected to fight alongside the Philistine troops, but David's reply was evasive: "Then you will see for yourself what your servant can do" (28: 2, NIV). The king interpreted this to mean, "Until now, you have received only verbal reports of the prowess of me and my men, but this battle will give us opportunity to display our skills before your very eyes." But is that what David meant? Certainly he wouldn't fight against his own people, and he probably had an alternate plan in mind. But the king was so impressed that he commissioned David to be his bodyguard for life![1]

The troops assembled and paraded, the five lords of the Philistines (6:16-17) leading their companies and David and his men bringing up the rear and guarding the king. When the princes (military commanders) of the Philistines saw their king with David and his 600, they protested, "What are these Hebrews doing here?" This question must have shocked Achish because he had the utmost confidence in David. He hastened to assure his commanders that he had watched David for over a year, in fact, from the first day David left Saul (21:10-15), and he trusted him.

The leaders couldn't argue with their king, but they could suggest a safety measure. They remembered that in a previous battle, some Hebrew soldiers in the Philistine army had deserted their posts and fought for Israel (14:21), and David and his men might do the same thing. True, Saul was David's enemy, but they might be reconciled and fight together. After all, the people used to sing, "Saul slew his thousands, and David his ten thousands" (28:5; 18:7; 21:11), which suggests that they were once fighting together. The safest thing to do was to send David back to Ziklag, far from the battle, and let him carry on his own military attacks elsewhere.

The king gave the message to David, who continued his deception by appearing to be deeply hurt by the order. Had he not proved himself to his king? He wanted to go out and "fight against the enemies of [his] lord, the king," another ambiguous statement that the king would interpret in his favor. But who was David's "lord and king"—King Saul (24:8; 26:17), Achish, or Jehovah? And who were David's enemies—the Jews or the Philistines? But Achish assumed that he was David's king, so he ordered him to quietly leave Gath and go back to Ziklag and not to upset the commanders in any way. They had a demanding battle ahead of them and Achish wanted them to be at their best. David obeyed and returned to Ziklag.[2]

Though the Lord was gracious to deliver David and his men from participating in this battle, He isn't obligated to step in and extricate His people from situations caused by their own sinful decisions. We reap what we sow, and in later years, David suffered from being deceived by members of his staff and even of his own family.

3. Delivering the captives (1 Sam. 30:1-20)
David and his band were kept from fighting with the Philistines, but they still had a battle to fight, this time with the Amalekites, the sworn enemies of the Lord and of the Jews (Ex. 17:8-16; Deut. 25:17). Because Saul had won an incomplete victory over the Amalekites (1 Sam. 15:1-11), they were still free to attack God's people.

Distress (1 Sam. 30:1-6a). Perhaps the Lord permitted this raid on Ziklag to encourage David to get out of enemy territory and go back to Judah where he belonged. The Amalekite leaders knew that David was at Gath and that all attention was focused on the confrontation between Israel and the Philistines. This was a perfect time to retaliate against David for his raids and to pick up some booty as well. Since most of the men were with David, the residents of Ziklag could put up no resistance and the invaders simply kidnapped the people and took whatever wealth they could find. They burned the city, an act of vengeance on their part but perhaps a message from the Lord that it was time for David to think about returning to Judah.

We can but imagine the horror and grief of David and his 600 men who had never lost a battle. Their city was burned, their wealth had been confiscated, and their wives and children had been kidnapped. It was the mercy of the Lord that the Amalekites spared the lives of the women and children, for in their raids David and his men had certainly killed their share of enemy women and children (27:11). The verb "carried them away" (30:2) is literally "drove them off" and paints the picture of animals being driven off by the herdsmen. The men wore themselves out in weeping and David was "greatly distressed," a verb that means he was pressed into a tight corner, the way a potter would press clay into a mold.

Encouragement (1 Sam. 30:6b-15). Different people react in different ways to the same circumstances, because what life does to us depends on what life finds in us. Some of the people wanted to stone David, which was certainly a foolish response. They needed their leader now more than ever, and how would his death solve their problem? We don't blame the men for being grieved, but we question their allowing their hearts to run ahead of their heads. David knew that the encouragement he needed could only come from the Lord. He ordered Abiathar the priest to bring the ephod and together they sought the will of the Lord. Saul had consulted the Lord but had received no answer (28:3-6), but the Lord graciously replied to David's request. David was hardly in a place of complete obedience, but God answered him just the same (Ps. 103:3-10).

Assured by the Lord that his pursuit of the enemy would meet with success, David and his men took off on their beasts and traveled sixteen miles to the brook Besor where 200 men had to stop because they were exhausted. (The Hebrew word translated "faint" means "dead tired.") That might have discouraged David, but he and his 400 men continued to travel. But where should they go? The Lord hadn't told them where the Amalekites were camped, but David trusted the Lord to guide him. It was then that they found an Egyptian slave whom his Amalekite master had abandoned because he was ill. The man could have perished in the wilderness, but the Lord had kept him alive for the sake of His servant David. The slave's master must have been an important man because his servant knew the plans of the Amalekite raiding party and could lead David to their camp. The master hoped that the man would die, but the Lord kept him alive so David could rescue the families that had been kidnapped.

Victory (1 Sam. 30:16-20). In their exuberant false confidence, the Amalekites were celebrating their great victory when David and his men attacked and caught the camp by surprise. They killed all the Amalekites, except 400 young men who escaped, rescued all the people who had been kidnapped, and recovered all the belongings that had been taken from Ziklag. It was a total victory for David, but it was also a profitable victory, because David took the wealth and booty of the Amalekites and claimed it for himself.

As you review what the Lord did for David in that dark hour in his life, you can better understand how He helps His people when problems and crises come into their lives. First, the Lord encouraged David so that he didn't despair but trusted the Lord to help him. Whenever a crisis comes, we need the courage to face it, and we must not try to blame others or pretend that nothing is wrong. The Lord also gave David wisdom to know what to do and the strength to do it. He and his men were weary, but the Lord enabled David and 400 of his men to persevere in their quest for the Amalekite invaders. The Lord also provided David with the facts he needed so he could find where the enemy was camping in that vast wilderness. When we step out by faith and trust the Lord, He will guide us when we need it. Finally, God gave David and his men the strength they needed to defeat the enemy and recover the prisoners and their wealth.

"Commit your way to the Lord, trust also in Him, and He shall bring it to pass" (Ps. 37:5).

4. Dividing the spoils (1 Sam. 30:21-31)

When David said to his troops, "This is David's spoil" (v. 20), he wasn't claiming the wealth of the Amalekites for himself in a selfish way but only stating that he would see to its distribution. Each of his fighting men received their part and so did the 200 soldiers who were too weary to continue the pursuit. This generosity of David bothered some of the "evil men and troublemakers" in David's band (v. 21), but David paid them no heed. He politely laid it down as a rule in his army that all the spoils would be divided among all the men, including those who didn't actually fight the enemy. After all, it was the Lord who gave them the victory, so nobody had the right to claim the spoils for himself as if the Lord owed it to him. God was gracious and generous to deliver the enemy into their hands, and they should be gracious and generous to share the wealth with others.

David also sent presents from the spoils to the elders of the towns in southern Judah, the places where he and his men had hidden during his wanderings (23:23). The people of these towns had helped David escape Saul, and David felt they deserved some kind of payment for their kindness. After all, if Saul had heard what they did, their very lives might have been in jeopardy. But David was doing more than thank these leaders. He was also paving the way for the time when he would return to their land as Israel's king

Even though the town had been burned by the enemy, David returned to Ziklag to await news of the battle between Israel and the Philistines. He was sure he wouldn't have to wait there very long, and he was right, for the news came on the third day (2 Sam. 1:1-2). After he heard the report of the death of Saul and his sons, he sought the Lord's guidance and the Lord sent him to Hebron (2:1-4). David reigned over Judah for seven and a half years, and Hebron was his capital city (v. 11).

The Lord had kept His promises, and David's wilderness wanderings were now ended.

The King is Dead!

First Samuel opens with the birth of a gifted baby, Samuel, and closes with the death of a guilty man, King Saul. The early chapters cluster around the tabernacle where God spoke to young Samuel, and the closing chapters focus on a forsaken man to whom God refused to speak. Samuel prayed and God defeated the Philistines; Saul sought for God's help but He didn't answer, and the Philistines defeated Israel. First Samuel is the book of man's king and is a record of Saul's decline, defeat, and death. Second Samuel is the record of God's king, David, and it shows how God made a mighty monarch out of a shepherd boy. King Saul's final days are recorded in these two chapters.

1. A night of deception and distress (1 Sam. 28:3-25)

Of all the "night scenes" in the Bible—and there are many of them—this one is perhaps the strangest and most dramatic. The spirit of a dead man returned to announce the doom of a despairing king who can find no way of escape. Samuel and Saul met for the last time, and it was not a happy meeting.

Saul didn't receive God's help (1 Sam. 28:3-6). We have already learned that Samuel was dead (25:1), but the fact is repeated here for perhaps two reasons. First, Israel was in trouble and Samuel wasn't there to rescue them as he had done before (7:7-14), and second, Saul was in trouble and Samuel wasn't there to give him God's counsel. When Samuel was alive, he had told Saul and the people what they needed to do to defeat the Philistines (7:3). However, their faith in God had gradually eroded under the leadership of King Saul, who was now deliberately seeking help from the evil one. It was Israel's darkest hour, but if God had deserted them, it was only because Saul had first deserted God.

The Philistine army was already mobilizing, and Saul and his army weren't prepared to meet them. When he saw them assembled, he became very frightened and trembled. The Philistines first gathered at Aphek while Israel assembled at Jezreel (29:1). Then the Philistines moved to Jezreel (v. 11) and finally to Shunem (28:4), where they prepared to attack the Israelite army stationed at Mount Gilboa (v. 4; 31:1).

Saul attempted to get in touch with the Lord through dreams, but there was no answer. He had no prophet with him, as David did (22:5), and David also had a priest with an ephod (23:6). The "Urim" mentioned in 28:6 must refer to a new ephod that somebody had made for Saul, because the ephod from the tabernacle was with David. No matter what means Saul tried, he received no answer from God.[1] But during most of his life, he didn't want God's will because he wanted to do things his own way. Is it any wonder that at the end of Saul's career, God deserted him?

"Then they will call on me, but I will not answer; they will seek me diligently, but they will not find me. Because they hated knowledge and did not choose the fear of the Lord, they would have none of my counsel and despised all my reproof, therefore they shall eat the fruit of their own way, and be filled to the full with their own fancies" (Prov. 1:28-31, NKJV).

Saul disobeyed God's Word (1 Sam. 28:7-14). The information in verse 3 about Saul putting away the people involved in spiritistic practices prepares us for the shock of Saul seeking for a spirit medium to assist him. The Law of Moses condemns all forms of spiritism (Ex. 22:18; Lev. 19:31; 20:6; Deut. 18:9-13), so Saul was right in having these people expelled, but he was wrong to seek their help. In doing so, he was both a deliberate sinner and a hypocrite. The fact that some of his servants knew where a spirit medium lived suggests that Saul's clean-up campaign wasn't too thorough and that not all of his officers agreed with him. Some of them knew a medium Saul had overlooked.

The night before the battle (1 Sam. 28:19), Saul disguised himself by taking off every sign of royalty and dressing in common clothes. He had a ten-mile journey from Mt. Gilboa to Endor and would pass very near the Philistine lines, so it wouldn't do to be recognized as the King of Israel. Furthermore, he didn't want the medium to know who he was. Saul began his reign at the dawning of the day when he was anointed king by Samuel the prophet (9:26), but he ended his reign by going out at night to visit a spirit medium. He broke the very law he attempted to enforce.

The woman was no fool. She wanted to be sure this wasn't a trap to catch her and condemn her, for spiritism was a capital crime in Israel. Saul took an oath using the name of the Lord whose law he was breaking, that she would not be prosecuted, so she agreed to cooperate. Saul not only violated the law himself, but he encouraged her to violate it! He asked her to get in contact with Samuel, the man Saul didn't want to contact when the prophet was alive.

He discovered God's plan (vv. 15-19). Taking the plain meaning of the text, it seems clear that Samuel did appear to the woman *but she was shocked when it happened.* Samuel didn't come up from the realm of the dead because she was a good medium but because the Lord willed it to happen. This was not a demon imitating Samuel, or the medium using clever tricks, otherwise the woman wouldn't have been shocked. Her surprised loud cry was evidence that Samuel's sudden appearing was something she didn't expect to happen. She saw the prophet but Saul didn't (vv. 13-14), but Samuel spoke directly to Saul and not through the medium. Samuel was a prophet of God and needed no "mouthpiece" to convey the Lord's message. In fact, verse 21 suggests that the woman was not close to Saul during the time Samuel delivered his message to the king.

Saul had only one question for Samuel: "What shall I do?" The Philistines were ready to attack, Saul was a weak and worried man, and everything he did to ascertain the Lord's will didn't work. "God is departed from me." Seven times in his brief message Samuel used the word "Lord" as he reminded Saul that God had departed from him because he refused to obey God's will. God tore the kingdom from Saul because he hadn't obeyed in the matter of slaying the Amalekites (15:28), and for the first time, Samuel announced that David was the "neighbor" who would inherit the kingdom (28:17). But the direst news of all was that the next day Saul and his sons would be slain in battle and join Samuel in the realm of the dead.[2]

Saul despaired over his plight (1 Sam. 28:20-25). The king was sitting on a couch next to the wall, and when he heard Samuel's words, he fell helpless, full length on the floor. He had wanted a message from the Lord, but when it came, it wasn't the message he wanted to hear. He was trembling with fear at hearing the announcement of his death, and he was weak from fasting. Why would a general fast before a strategic battle? Was Saul trying to buy help from the Lord as he had done once before? (14:28) Some authorities believe that mediums required people to fast before they came to a séance, so perhaps Saul had that in mind. In either case, his actions were foolish, because fasting can't earn the blessing of the Lord if the heart isn't right with God.

The medium shifted into a motherly role and begged the king to eat something. He had a dangerous journey ahead of him back to his camp, and the next day he had to direct his troops in the battle against the Philistines. As he had foolishly done before, Saul tried to "play the man" and appear the hero, substituting bravado for sanity, but the pleas of the medium and Saul's men prevailed. The woman must have been fairly well to do to have a fattened calf readily available, because this was the diet of the wealthy and a rare delicacy for the common people. Indeed, it was a meal fit for a king, but it was also his "last supper" before leaving this life. Saul ate and then left the medium's house. The final statement in the chapter reminds us of Judas—"He then having received the sop went immediately out: and it was night" (John 13:30, KJV).

We can't help but feel sorry for Saul, and yet at the same time, we must admit that he brought his plight on himself. Had he obeyed the Lord he wouldn't have lost the kingdom, and had he stopped pursuing David and invested his time developing his army, he would have been better equipped to meet the Philistines at Jezreel. In spite of all the blessings God gave to Saul, and all the opportunities to grow spiritually, Saul was unprepared to lead, unprepared to fight, and unprepared to die.

2. A day of disgrace and defeat (1 Sam. 31:1-10; 1 Chron. 10)
Saul's military record is summarized in 1 Samuel 14:47-48. It's a commendable record that presents Saul as a conquering general and a national hero. He began his career as a great success; after all, the people did sing, "Saul has slain his thousands." It was after his failure to destroy the Amalekites that Saul began to go downhill. When David came on the scene, Saul's envy of the young man's success so obsessed him that the king became paranoid and dangerous. Saul had many good qualities, but none of them was humble, obedient faith in God. Because of his pride and disobedience, Saul lost everything.

Saul lost his army (1 Sam. 31:1; 1 Chron. 10:1). Saul's soldiers were no match for the Philistine army with its large divisions and its many chariots. Some of the men deserted and many others died on the battlefield. The Philistines preferred to fight on level ground because they depended on their chariots, while Israel tried to lure them into the hill country around Mount Gilboa. Israel was outnumbered and outclassed, but even if they had boasted superior forces, they still would have been defeated. Saul's hour of judgment had come. Without Samuel's prayers and David's anointed leadership, the army of Israel was destined for defeat.

Saul lost his life (1 Sam. 31:2-7; 1 Chron. 10:1-6). One of the first rules of ancient warfare was, "Kill the enemy king!" (See 1 Kings 22:31.) Saul was on the field with three of his four sons; for some reason, Ish-Bosheth (also known as Esh-Baal) was missing (2 Sam. 2:8; 1 Chron. 8:33; 9:39). The three sons died first, and then Saul was fatally struck by an arrow and asked his armor-bearer to kill him. The Philistines were notorious at abusing and humiliating victims, especially officers and kings. Saul feared that he would be tortured to death, so when the young man failed to respond to his plea, he fell on his sword and died.[3] The young man immediately took his own life, and eventually all of Saul's bodyguards and officers around him met their death. It was total victory for the Philistines.

Saul's reign was a tragic one and his death seemed inevitable, but how sad that three of his sons should die with him on the battlefield. Jonathan had dreamed of being coregent with David (1 Sam. 23:16-18), but that dream was never fulfilled. How often the sins of one bring pain and even death to others. "There is a sin leading to death" (1 John 5:16, NKJV). The sins of both Saul and Eli (4:1-18) cost them their lives and the lives of their sons. God is no respecter of persons.

Saul lost his honor (1 Sam. 31:8-10; 1 Chron. 10:8-10). Humiliating the prisoners and the dying and stripping the dead,were the chief activities of a victorious army, for the spoils of battle were a big part of their wages for risking their lives. The Philistines took great joy in abusing Saul's body. They stripped off his armor and cut off his head, and after parading both from place to place in their land (1 Chron. 10:9), they displayed them in their temples. The armor was put in the temple of their goddess Ashtareth, and the head in the temple of Dagon. Finally, they publicly displayed the mutilated corpses of Saul and his sons on the outside of the city wall of Bethshan, a Philistine controlled city in the Jezreel Valley. For a Jew not to receive proper burial was both humiliating and sacrilegious, and for the body to be mutilated and then exposed was even more scandalous. The Philistines were letting their people and their idols know that they had won a great victory over their chief enemy, the people of Israel. Dagon had triumphed over Jehovah!

Saul lost his crown (2 Sam. 1:1-10). The account of Saul's death given to David by the Amalekite was primarily a lie. The man "happened" to be at the battle but was obviously there to steal loot, and he had taken the two insignias of royalty from Saul's dead body. He had not put Saul out of his misery because Saul had committed suicide and was dead when the man arrived. After removing the royal crown and bracelet, the Amalekite, (who may have been a mercenary in one of the armies) should have safely removed the body from the field and protected it until it could have proper burial. He thought that his heroic acts would win David's approval, but they only brought him death.

Because of his sins, Saul first lost his dynasty (13:11-14) and then his kingdom (15:24-31), and finally he lost his crown. The warning of our Lord in Revelation 3:11 is applicable at this point: "Behold, I come quickly! Hold fast what you have, that no one may take your crown" (NKJV). "Look to yourselves, that we do not lose those things we worked for, but that we may receive a full reward" (2 John 8, NKJV).

3. An hour of daring and devotion (1 Sam. 31:11-13; 1 Chron. 10:11-13)

While the Philistines were making merry over defeating Israel and humiliating Saul and his sons, the men of Jabesh Gilead heard about the tragedy and came to the rescue. King Saul's first great victory had been the delivering of Jabesh Gilead from the Ammonites (1 Sam. 11:1-11), so the people of the city felt an obligation to vindicate Saul's memory. All of their valiant men traveled fifteen to twenty miles at night to the city of Bethshan and took possession of the four mutilated and decaying bodies. In order to make this trip, they had to cross the Jordan River and go through enemy territory. Saul hadn't been a spiritual leader, but he was a courageous leader and the first king of Israel. Even if we can't respect the man, we must show respect for the office.

The men risked their lives a second time and carried the bodies to Jabesh Gilead. There they burned the bodies to remove the mutilated and decayed flesh, and they left the bones for burial. They didn't cremate the bodies, because cremation wasn't a Jewish practice. In times of emergency, the Jews would burn corpses that were so mutilated and decayed they couldn't be properly washed and anointed for burial; and then they would give honorable burial to the bones. After the people of Jabesh Gilead buried the bones, they fasted for seven days. It was their tribute to Saul and his sons.

Saul had often held court under a tree in Ramah (22:6), and now he was buried with three of his sons under a tree near Jabesh Gilead. Later, David disinterred the bones of Saul and Jonathan and had them buried in their family's tomb in Benjamin (2 Sam. 21:13-14).

THIRTEEN

REVIEW OF 1 SAMUEL

Four Successes and Two Failures

When the American statesman Benjamin Franklin signed the "Declaration of Independence" on July 4, 1776, he remarked, "We must indeed all hang together, or most assuredly, we shall all hang separately." The road from signing a document to achieving national unity was a long one and a costly one, but eventually the United States of America emerged on the political scene and has been there ever since. Its two mottoes summarize the miracle that was accomplished: "E pluribus unum—Out of many, one" and "In God we trust." The first tells us what happened and the second tells us how it happened.

The nation of Israel had a similar challenge. After the death of Joshua, Israel gradually became a divided nation. Instead of trusting the Lord, the Jews began to worship the gods of their pagan neighbors, and the spiritual bonds that held the tribes together began to weaken and break. Before long, people were doing what was right in their own eyes and caring little about the covenant they had made with the Lord. Then the people called for a king, for someone who could bring unity to the nation and victory to the army. God answered their request and gave them Saul, but not to solve their problems—he only made some of them worse—but to prove to the people that their greatest need was to trust in Him and obey His Word. It wasn't until David appeared on the scene that national events began to take a different turn and light appeared at the end of the tunnel.

David was anointed by Samuel, and Samuel was the son of Elkanah and Hannah; so the story begins with Hannah, a humble woman whose submission and faith in God are an example for all of us to follow.

1. Hannah, a godly woman

The name Hannah means "grace," and she certainly lived up to her name. God gave her the grace she needed to suffer the insults hurled at her by Peninnah, Elkanah's second wife, and to endure the embarrassment and pain of childlessness. She received the grace she needed to speak kindly and gently when she was misunderstood and criticized (Col. 4:6). God gave her grace to conceive a son and dedicate him to the Lord—and then to sing about it! So beautiful and meaningful was Hannah's song that Mary borrowed from it when she praised the Lord for His grace to her (Luke 1:46-55).

Hannah was a woman with "faith and patience" (Heb. 6:12) who committed herself to God, asked for a son, and waited for God to answer in His own way and time. She was patient at home as she endured the verbal attacks of Peninnah, and she was patient with Eli when he falsely accused her of being drunk. She was fortunate to have a devout husband who loved her and encouraged her to obey the Lord. There were times when life was very difficult for Hannah, but she persevered in her faith, hope, and love and eventually won the victory.

Hannah realized what too many of us forget, that God works in and through "common people" to accomplish His purposes on earth. He didn't ask Hannah to lead an army, as He did Deborah (Jud. 4–5), or intercede with a king, as He did Esther. He simply asked her to fulfill her heart's desire and give birth to a son. "Delight yourself also in the Lord, and He shall give you the desires of your heart" (Ps. 37:4). All that Hannah wanted was to be a woman of God who obeyed the will of God. In doing this, she helped to save the nation of Israel.

There's so much treachery, bloodshed, and confusion recorded in 1 Samuel that it's refreshing to meet at the very beginning of the book a woman who represents the very best that God has to give. The leaders of Israel had failed, so God sought out a woman He could use to help bring truth, peace, and order to His people. She served God simply by being a woman and doing what only a woman could do—give birth to a baby and dedicate that child to the Lord.

"He settles the barren woman in her home as a happy mother of children. Praise the Lord" (Ps. 113:9, NIV).

2. Eli, a compromising priest

Eli was an indulgent father who occasionally reproved his sons for their sins but took no steps to discipline the men, let alone replace them. The work at the tabernacle went on in a routine sort of way, but there was no spiritual power evident nor was there any fresh word from the Lord. The picture we get of Eli is that of a fat, old man, sitting on his special chair as he directed the affairs of the tabernacle, all the while closing his eyes to what he saw and his ears to what he heard. He was the leader of Israel's religion and desperately needed to have a fresh experience with the Lord.

But we can commend Eli for putting his blessing on Hannah's prayer request (1 Sam. 1:17) and for welcoming little Samuel when she brought him to be dedicated to the Lord. Samuel's sons weren't the best companions for an innocent little boy, but the Lord and Eli saw to it that Samuel wasn't defiled. Eli taught Samuel the truths of God Word and instructed him concerning the work and ways of the tabernacle. Samuel was born a priest, but God would call him to minister as a prophet and judge.

Something else is commendable in Eli: when the Lord sent His message to young Samuel, Eli counseled the boy, listened to the message, and submitted to the Lord's will. "It is the Lord. Let Him do what seems good to Him" (3:18, NKJV). Whether this statement was a confession of helpless resignation or a mark of worshipful submission isn't easy to determine, but let's give Eli the benefit of the doubt. As he saw God at work in young Samuel's life, Eli must have encouraged him and prayed for him. There's no record that he was envious of the lad because God's messages were coming through him. Blessed are those older saints who help the new generation know God and live for Him! However Eli may have failed with his own sons, he helped to point Samuel in the right direction and the whole nation benefited from it.

Eli's last day of ministry was a tough one: his two sons died, the ark was captured by the enemy, and his daughter-in-law died giving birth to a son. "Ichabod—the glory has departed!" But God was still on the throne and young Samuel was getting ready to step into the gap and bring spiritual direction to the nation. Eli hadn't been a great spiritual leader, but he was one small link in the chain that led to the anointing of David and eventually the birth of the Redeemer.

3. Samuel, a faithful servant

Samuel was born at a time when the nation and its religion were a stagnant pool, but he soon found himself trying to navigate on a stormy sea. Change was in the air, and priests were trained to protect tradition, not to promote alteration. The Jewish leaders wanted a king, someone who could unify the people and protect them from the surrounding nations. Samuel saw this move as an abandonment of the Kingship of Jehovah, but the Lord told him to go along with the people and anoint Saul as king. Samuel did his best to educate the people for life under a monarchy, but his words seemed to make little difference

The people had voted Samuel out of his judgeship, but he was still God's priest and prophet, and he helped Saul get a good start. Samuel led the nation in renewing their covenant with the Lord, Saul rescued the people of Jabesh Gilead, and Samuel gave a moving farewell speech in which he promised to pray for the nation. But it soon became evident that Saul had very little spiritual discernment and that he was using the kingship to promote himself, not to assist the people. He lied about his willful disobedience, lost the kingdom, and sent Samuel home to Ramah with a broken heart.

Real change agents don't sit around complaining and remembering the good old days. When God told Samuel to go to Bethlehem and anoint a new king, he risked his life and obeyed, and David became a part of the scene. Scripture doesn't tell us how much mentoring Samuel gave David, but the prophet recognized God's hand on the lad and surely taught him about the Lord and His people. Samuel was God's living link between Israel's past and future, and he played his part well. He befriended David when he was in danger, prayed for him, and trusted God to care for him.

Samuel is an example to all older believers who are prone to glorify the past, resist change in the present, and lose hope in the future. Without abandoning the past, Samuel accepted change, did all he could to make things work, and when they didn't work, trusted God for a brighter future. God didn't abandon the kingdom; He just chose a better man to be in charge, and Samuel helped to mentor that man. Every leader needs a Samuel, a person in touch with God, appreciative of the past but willing to follow God into a new era, a man of faith and encouragement who sees the hand of God at work where others see only confusion.

Nobody could buy Samuel's conscience or accuse him of putting money ahead of ministry. The only blot on his record is the covetousness of his sons who used their ministry to line their own pockets. Nothing is said in Scripture about Samuel's wife, so perhaps she died young and this deprived the boys of her godly instruction and example. Samuel was often away from home, covering his ministry circuit, and this may have left the boys too much to themselves. It's useless to second-guess history. But after seeing what Samuel did for David, we can perhaps forgive what he didn't do for his own sons.

4. Saul, an unstable king

Saul's chief problem seemed to be his lack of a spiritual foundation on which to build a godly life. He may have stood head and shoulders above everybody else, but he was a midget when he stood next to David or even his son Jonathan. This lack of spiritual experience resulted in a second deficiency—a lack of confidence in himself and in the Lord. This had to be covered up by a leadership style that fed his ego and kept everybody around him in fear. At the start of his reign, when he was supposed to be encouraging the people, he was hiding in the baggage! Yet during his reign, he kept his spear constantly with him, not just to protect himself but also to remind everybody who was boss. He believed any lie about David that would give him reason to rally the troops and forget the needs of the nation.

When David arrived on the scene, he didn't create problems—he revealed them. An insecure man like Saul can't tolerate competition and competence, and this made David an enemy. The people loved David and honored him, and this only made Saul's paranoia grow faster. Saul became a double-minded man who was "unstable in all his ways" (James 1:8). On the one hand, he pursued David and tried to kill him, while on the other hand he wept when he saw David or heard his voice, and tried to appear apologetic and repentant. His was the shallow heart of our Lord's Parable of the Sower. There was no depth, the tears were temporary, and no lasting fruit ever appeared.

Paradoxical as it seems, it was *success* that helped to bring about Saul's ruin. Charles de Gaulle, president of France, said, "Success contains within it the germs of failure, and the reverse is also true." Those germs of failure are planted by the hands of pride, and pride was one of Saul's besetting sins. He was suddenly forced out of the predictable work of a farmer and herdsman into the unpredictable work of a king, and he didn't have the equipment to work with. The Lord would have helped him, as he did Moses, Joshua, and Gideon, but Saul chose to go his own way. When success comes before we're ready for it, it can destroy us and rob us of the things that make for true success. Saul didn't know the difference.

When Saul failed, he learned to substitute excuses for confessions, but his lies only entangled him worse. His life and royal service were part of a tragic masquerade that was applauded by his flatterers and abominated by the Lord. Saul didn't listen to Moses, Samuel, Jonathan, or David, and once he had rejected God's Word, the only voice left was that of the devil.

"I know of no more unhappy character than Saul when God had departed from him," said Charles Haddon Spurgeon. "But, somehow, there was not the anguish in the soul of Saul that there would have been if he had ever really known the Lord. I do not think that he ever did really, in his inmost soul, know the Lord. After Samuel anointed him, he was 'turned into another man,' but he never became a new man. . . ."[1] Campbell Morgan said, "The man in his government of Israel was a warrior and nothing more; he was never a shepherd."[2] He held a spear, not a shepherd's crook.

When God calls people to serve, He knows their capacity for doing the work He wants them to do, and He will never abandon them—if they trust and obey. That's where Saul failed. When God is left out of the equation, the answer is always zero.

Centuries later, another Saul appeared on the scene—Saul of Tarsus, who quickly became known as Paul, "the small one."[3] He said he was "less than the least of all saints" (Eph. 3:8), which is quite a contrast to the Old Testament Saul with his great stature and manly physique. King Saul died a suicide on the battlefield, but his namesake died a martyr outside the city of Rome. Before his death, he wrote to his beloved Timothy, "I have fought a good fight, I have finished my course, I have kept the faith" (2 Tim. 4:7).

Ten seconds after he died, King Saul wished he could have said those words.

5. Jonathan, a generous friend

British preacher and composer George Matheson was right when he called Jonathan "a rainbow in a storm."[4] You don't find

Jonathan speaking a pessimistic word or questioning God's ability to accomplish what had to be done. He and his armor-bearer challenged the Philistine outpost and won. He openly defied his father's bizarre instructions and taught his fellow soldiers a lesson in sane military manners. Jonathan risked his life to help David escape and then went to him in his exile so he could encourage him. The natural heir to the throne, Jonathan stripped himself of his royal garments and his armor and gave them to David.

Jonathan didn't mind being second man. He loved David and love always puts other people first. Jonathan made a covenant with David to become coregent when David ascended the throne, a promise, alas, that David couldn't fulfill. Jonathan loved his father and his nation to the very end and died on the battlefield while trying to defend king and country. It's tragic that so noble a prince should die because of the poor leadership displayed by his father, but God didn't want Saul's line and David's line together in the throne room.

Jonathan leaves behind a beautiful example of what true friendship should be: honest, loving, sacrificing, seeking the welfare of others, and always bringing hope and encouragement when the situation is difficult. Jonathan never achieved a crown on earth, but he certainly received one in heaven. "Be faithful until death, and I will give you the crown of life" (Rev. 2:10).

6. David, a courageous shepherd

The eighth son and the "baby" of the family, David should have lived and died in anonymity, but he was a man after God's own heart, and God put His hand upon him. It's too bad that when his name is mentioned, people instantly remember his sin with Bathsheba and the murder of her husband, because, as terrible as those sins were, David was a great man and served God in a great way. We ought also to remember the way he built and protected the kingdom of Israel, or the many psalms he wrote, or the sacrifices he made on the battlefield to gather wealth for the building of the temple. God forgave David and David paid dearly for his sins, but God never cast David aside or refused his dedicated service. "So then each of us shall give account of himself to God" (Rom. 14:12, NKJV).

David was a man athirst for God. He envied the priests because they were privileged to dwell in God's house and live close to His presence. But He saw God in the mountains and rivers as much as in the sanctuary, and he heard God's voice in the thunder. For David, the world was alive with God, and the highest honor one could have—higher than being king—was to be God's servant and accomplish His purposes on earth.

God first trained David in solitude as he cared for the flock, and when the time was right, He thrust him on the stage and trained him even more in suffering. Some of his brothers criticized him, his king tried to kill him, and the king's courtiers lied about him, but David lived his life open before the Lord and never turned back. No, he wasn't perfect, nor did he claim to be, but his heart was fixed, and his consuming desire was to glorify God and finish his work.

Though on occasion he wavered because of doubts, David believed God's promises and never turned back in unbelief. Doubt is a temporary relapse of the heart, but unbelief is a permanent rebellion of the will, and David was never guilty of that. Even during his sojourns in enemy territory, he sought ways to accomplish something that would further God's kingdom.

David was a unique blending of soldier and shepherd, musician and military tactician, commander and commoner. In spite of his sins and failures—and we all have them—he was Israel's greatest king, and always will be until King Jesus reigns on David's throne as Prince of Peace. The next time we're tempted to emphasize the negative things in David's life, let's remember that Jesus wasn't ashamed to be called "the Son of David."

Four successes: Hannah, a housewife; Samuel, a prophet and priest; Jonathan, a prince and friend; and David, a shepherd.

Two failures: Eli, a priest, and Saul, a king.

And the Lord still says to us, "Let Jesus be king of your life. Be successful!"

NOTES

Chapter 1

1. Ramah means "height" and Ramathaim means "the two heights." A number of cities had "ramah" in their names (Josh 13:26; 19:29; 21:38; Jud. 4:5; 1 Sam. 30:27), but it's likely that Elkanah and his family lived in Ramathaim ("double heights") on the border of Benjamin and Ephraim. Elkanah was a Levite by birth but an Ephraimite by residence.

2. The NIV and NASB both read "a double portion" and the NLT says "a special portion," but some students translate 1:5 "only one portion." It seems, however, that Elkanah was trying to show special love to his wife at a difficult time, so the gift must have been special.

3. Psalm 99:6 and Jeremiah 15:1 identify Samuel as a man of prayer, and he's named in Hebrews 11:32 as a man of faith. For instances of special prayer on his part, see 1 Samuel 7:8-9; 8:6; 12:18-19, 23; 15:11.

4. In her brief speech recorded in 1:25-28, Hannah frequently used different forms of the Hebrew word *sa-al*, which means "asked" and is a basis for the name "Samuel." The word "lent" in v. 28 (KJV) means "given." Hannah's surrender of Samuel to the Lord was final.

5. Of course, the earth isn't resting on the tops of pillars. This is poetic language based on the architecture of that day. See also Job 38:4; Psalm 75:3; 82:5; 104:5; Isaiah 24:18.

6. There is no record in Scripture how the high priesthood moved from Eleazar's line to Ithamar's and hence eventually to Eli.

7. The priests who serve in the temple during the Kingdom Age will be from the family of Zadok (Ezek. 40:45-46; 43:19; 44:10-16).

8. The repetition of names when God speaks is also found when the Lord spoke to Abraham (Gen. 22:11), Moses (Ex. 3:4), Martha (Luke 10:41), and Paul (Acts 9:4; 26:14).

9. Samuel would have a ministry of "opening doors" for others. He opened the doors of kingship to Saul, who failed to use it for God's glory, and also to David, who used his position to serve God and the people. Samuel established a school of the prophets and opened doors

of ministry to the men God sent to him. He opened the doors to a new beginning for the nation of Israel that was at low ebb both spiritually and politically.

Chapter 2

1. Obviously 1 Samuel was written after the events described, so the name "Ebenezer" is used here by anticipation. See 1 Samuel 7:12. However, it may have been another site with the same name.

2. The word "hand" is a key word in this story. The "hand of the enemy" is found in 4:3; 7:3, 8. The Philistines spoke about "the hand of these mighty gods" (4:8), and "the hand of the Lord" is mentioned in 5:6-7, 9, 11; 6:3, 5, 9; and 7:13.

3. The Hebrew word *kabod* shows up frequently in this account. It means "heavy" but also can mean "honor, glory, respectful" (people of "weight"). Eli was "heavy" but he wasn't "weighty" when it came to character and godliness, what Paul called the "weight of glory" (1 Cor. 4:17).

4. Rachel named her second son "Ben-oni," which means "son of my sorrow," but Jacob changed it to Benjamin" which means "son of my right hand" (Gen. 35:16-18).

Chapter 3

1. The pouring out of the water could also be seen as a drink offering, symbolizing total devotion to the Lord, for liquids poured out can't be recovered again. See Psalm 62:8; Lamentations 2:19; Philippians 2:17; 2 Timothy 4:6. The only official fast on the Jewish calendar was on the Day of Atonement, but that didn't prevent the people from fasting at other times. The situation was critical, and the nation needed to "come clean" with the Lord.

2. The nation of Israel rejected God the Father when they asked for a king, God the Son when they said, "We have no king but Caesar" (John 19:15), and God the Holy Spirit when they stoned Stephen (Acts 7:51-60).

3. Going "back to Bethel" signifies a return to the Lord. Abraham did it (12:8; 13:1-4) and so did Jacob (Gen. 28:18-19; 35:1ff).

4. *The Westminster Pulpit* (London: Pickering and Inglis, n.d), vol. 9, 14.

Chapter 4

1. The Hebrew letters for *r* and *d* and *k* and *n* are very similar and someone copying a Hebrew manuscript could easily make a mistake. The original manuscripts of the Scriptures are inspired and inerrant, but minor spelling and numerical errors could creep into the copies.

2. The Hebrew text of 1 Samuel 13:1 reads, "Saul was a son of a year in his reigning, and he reigned two years over Israel," a perplexing statement indeed. The NIV reads "Saul was thirty years old when he became king, and he reigned over Israel forty-two years," but these numbers are not in the original text. The NASB says he was forty years old when he started his reign and was king for thirty-two years, but, again, these numbers are pure conjecture. The KJV settles for "Saul reigned one year; and when he had reigned two years over Israel Saul chose him three thousand men" (13:1-2). Paul said that Saul reigned forty years (Acts 13:21). Since Saul's son Jonathan was old enough to be a commander in the army, Saul could well have been forty or older when he became king. If he reigned thirty years, he would have been seventy when he died. Some chronologists have conjectured that Saul was born in 1080 and became king in 1050 at age thirty. If Saul died at age seventy, that would have been in 1010. See *The Expositor's Bible Commentary*, vol. 3, 373, for Ronald F. Youngblood's suggested chronology. Obviously, not all Old Testament students agree, and this is understandable because the factual data are not complete. No doctrinal matter is affected by this problem.

3. Like the Latin, the Hebrew language uses letters to represent numbers, so it was easy for copyists to make errors. Some students believe that "30,000 chariots" is a scribal error and that the number should be 3,000. The *l* at the end of Israel could have been copied twice, and this would have turned "three" into "thirty." In ancient warfare, the number of cavalry soldiers always exceeded the number of charioteers, and the Philistines mustered 6,000 cavalrymen. But regardless of the exact numbers, the Jewish army was definitely outnumbered by the enemy.

4. Saul called himself a fool in 1 Sam. 26:21, and David admitted he had done foolishly when he numbered the people (2 Sam. 24:10; 1 Chron. 21:8). However, David was sincere in his confession and truly

repented of his sin. In 2 Chronicles 16:9, the seer Hanani told King Asa he had done a foolish thing in robbing God's temple in order to hire heathen soldiers to fight his battles. All disobedience to God is folly and leads ultimately to failure and pain.

Chapter 5

1. Jonathan's "test" wasn't an act of unbelief as was Gideon's fleece (Jud. 6:36-40). Jonathan already had the faith he needed to defeat the enemy, but he wanted to know how the Lord wanted him to attack. It's wrong for God's children to "put out the fleece" and set up conditions that God has to meet before they will obey Him. Sometimes the Lord stoops to our level of weakness and meets our conditions, but the practice doesn't build one's faith.

2. The phrase "bring the ark" in verse 18 is unusual, because the ark wasn't used for determining the will of God. "Bring the ephod" is what we expect to read, as in 1 Samuel 23:9 and 30:7. The ephod was that part of the high priest's official garments in which the Urim and Thummim were kept (Ex. 28:6-30). They were used to determine the will of God.

3. Twice Pharaoh said "I have sinned" (Ex. 9:27; 10:16), but his words were empty. As soon as the situation improved in Egypt, he went right back to opposing Moses and God. Balaam said, "I have sinned" (Num. 22:34) but continued to be an enemy of Israel. Judas admitted his sin but never really repented (Matt. 27:4). David said, "I have sinned" and really meant it (2 Sam. 12:13; 24:10, 17; Ps. 51:4), and so did the prodigal son (Luke 15:18, 21).

4. When the Bible speaks about the Lord "changing His mind" or "repenting," it is using human language to describe divine truth. God knows the future, including our responses to His commands, and God is never at a loss to know what to do. He does change His actions in response to what people do, but this has nothing to do with His changeless nature or attributes. Jonah announced that Nineveh would be destroyed, but the city repented and the Lord withdrew the judgment. From the human point of view, God seemed to change His mind, but not from the divine point of view. God is always true to His nature and consistent with His attributes and plans. Nothing catches Him by surprise

Chapter 6

1. The Hebrew word translated "youngest" in verse 11 also means "smallest." Saul was famous for his height (9:2; 10:23), but David was not conspicuous in the crowd. From the beginning of his ministry, David was seen as a man with a humble spirit.

2. Early in his life, David acknowledged that Jehovah God was King (Ps. 59:13). Blessed is that leader who recognizes that he is second in command!

3. Noah was "the eighth person" (2 Peter 2:5) and eight persons were saved in the ark to give a new beginning to civilization (1 Peter 3:20). Jewish boys were circumcised on the eighth day, which gave them a new status in the nation as "sons of the covenant," and the first-born were dedicated to God on the eighth day (Ex. 22:29-30).

4. In the Old Testament, the Spirit of God came upon people whom the Lord called to accomplish certain purposes for God, but He might also leave them as He did Saul. This fact helps to explain David's prayer in Psalm 51:11. Believers today who share in the New Covenant are assured that they have the Spirit forever (John 14:16). True believers are sealed by the Spirit at conversion, and the seal speaks of permanent possession and protection (Eph. 1:13-14 and 4:30).

5. Some chronologists calculate that David was born about 1085 and was anointed in 1070 at the age of fifteen or sixteen. Five years later (1065) he fled from Saul and was in exile for the next ten years. In 1055, he was crowned king over Judah when he was thirty years old (2 Sam. 2).

6. Fear seems to have been a constant problem with Saul. See 13:11; 15:24; 17:11; 18:12; 28:5. Faith and fear don't lodge in the same heart (Matt. 8:26).

7. Was the giant wearing his helmet or was he so confident that he left it behind? But even a helmet couldn't keep a heaven-impelled stone from penetrating Goliath's skull. It's likely that Goliath was in a combat posture, bent slightly forward and approaching David, and this plus the weight of his armor caused him to fall face forward.

8. The phrase "Israel and Judah" in verse 52, found also in 15:4, suggests that Saul didn't have a unified nation or a united army. Apparently the royal tribe of Judah operated as a separate entity. After

the death of Saul and his sons, it was the tribe of Judah that welcomed David as their king (2 Sam. 2:1-4).

9. Some Old Testament scholars think that David wrote Psalm 8 in honor of God's victory over Goliath. Both 1 Samuel 17 and Ps. 8 emphasize the name of God, the fowl of the air, and beasts of the field, and God's willingness to care for and use frail man.

Chapter 7

1. To make anything more out of their friendship than the mature affection of two manly believers is to twist the Scriptures. Had there been anything unlawful in their relationship, the Lord certainly would never have blessed David and protected him, and David could never have written Psalm 18:19-27 ten years later.

2. Merab and her husband had five sons, all of whom were sacrificed by the Gibeonites in order to end a famine in the land (2 Sam. 21:1-9).

3. The phrase "David's men" is found frequently in the Samuel narrative (18:27; 23:3-5; 24:3; 25:12-13). It seems that some of his soldiers stayed with him and became his "crack troops" during the days of his exile. They considered it a high honor to be known as "David's men," and indeed it was.

4. The shedding of innocent blood was a very serious crime in Israel. The six cities of refuge were set apart so that innocent people involved in manslaughter might not be treated as murderers (Deut. 19:1-10), and the ritual of the red heifer atoned for innocent blood shed by unknown murderers (Deut. 21:1-9). God hates the sin of shedding innocent blood (Prov. 6:16-17) and the prophets cried out against it (Isa. 59:7; Jer. 7:6; 22:17; 26:15). This was one of the sins that brought about the downfall in Jerusalem and the kingdom of Judah (2 Kings 21:16).

5. The goats' hair reminds us of Jacob's deceiving his father, Gen. 27:15-16. Surely Michal knew the story.

Chapter 8

1. David often mentioned in his psalms that his life was constantly in danger because people wanted to kill him: Psalms 34:4; 38:12; 40:14; 54:3; 63:9; 70:2. Psalm 18 summarizes David's ten years in exile and

how the Lord sustained and helped him.

2. It seems that David had a special hiding place that only Jonathan knew about, the place by the stone Ezel where David hid when all his trouble with Saul began (19:2; 20:19, NIV). The Hebrew word *ezel* means "the departure," a significant thing when you realize that it was there that David and Jonathan departed from each other and David departed from the service of Saul.

3. Jonathan's promise that he will tell David the truth almost sounds like he is minimizing his father's hatred for David (vv. 12-13). Even the NIV translation doesn't change this impression: "If he is favorably disposed toward you. But if my father is inclined to harm you. . . ." Perhaps we should expect a son to be more sanguine about his father's temper than the victim of the abuse, but Jonathan soon found out that Saul would kill him, too, if he could.

4. Jonathan's words "The Lord be between me and thee" must not be equated with the agreement between Laban and Jacob (Gen. 31:43-53), the so-called "Mizpah benediction," which is not a benediction at all. David and Jonathan trusted God and each other and knew that God would care for them and fulfill His purposes. Laban and Jacob didn't trust each other and reminded each other that the Lord would watch them and make sure neither one would cross the boundary to attack the other.

5. Biblical scholars don't agree on the authenticity of all the historical inscriptions to the psalms, but the psalms that have no inscriptions present an even greater mystery. In this book, I assume that the inscriptions are accurate.

6. The fact that Jesus mentioned Abiathar and not Ahimelech may come from the fact that Abiathar was the only priest who survived the slaughter that Saul commanded.

7. The Philistines called David "king" because they knew how popular he was with the people of Israel. He was the "king" of the battlefield.

8. The word "Ramah" in the KJV (v. 6) means "height," and therefore the NIV translates the text "on the hill at Gibeah." It's obvious that Saul and his officers couldn't be in Gibeah and Ramah at the same time, even though the cities were less than five miles apart.

9. Saul had enlisted everybody to help him locate David and used bribery and intimidation to get results (23:7, 19, 25, 27; 24:1; 26:1).

10. The *New Living Translation* uses the verb "shouted" in verses 7, 11 and 16.

11. The KJV translation of verse 15 suggests that this wasn't the first time the high priest had consulted the Lord for David, and the NIV backs this up. But there is no indication that David had ever gone to Nob to ask the high priest to determine God's will for him, including the occasion described by Doeg. David was merely a civil servant in Saul's employ and had no right to ask the high priest to inquire for him. Later, when Abiathar escaped and joined David's band, he did use the ephod to seek the Lord's will.

12. Unfortunately, Abiathar sided with Adonijah in his quest for the throne, and Solomon replaced him with Azariah from the priestly family of Zadok. This was the final step in eliminating Eli's family from the levitical priesthood.

Chapter 9

1. David himself was called a prophet (2 Sam. 23:2; Acts 4:25), but this gift seems to have been used primarily in the writing of the Psalms, especially those that speak about the Messiah.

2. David had a double claim on the people of Ziph: he was their brother, a member of the tribe of Judah, and he was their deliverer.

3. In the superscription to Psalm 18, David separated Saul from his enemies.

4. Saul was sure that the Lord had delivered David into his hands (23:7), and David's men were sure the Lord had delivered Saul into David's hands! It all depends on your point of view!

5. David used a familiar proverb that is now a part of Scripture, but that doesn't mean that folksy proverbs carry the same authority as the inspired Word of God. There is practical wisdom in some proverbs, but they have a tendency to contradict one another. "Look before you leap" is balanced by "He who hesitates is lost," and "Absence makes the heart grow fonder" by "Out of sight, out of mind."

6. The writer may have seen in this question a reflection of Isaac's words to Jacob, who was impersonating Esau, "Are you really my son

Esau?" (Gen. 27:24, NKJV). Yet it was Saul who was the liar, not David.

Chapter 10

1. This is not Mount Carmel, located far north on the border of Asher and Manasseh, near the Mediterranean Sea.

2. Caleb's family tree is found in 1 Chronicles 2:18-54, and it's interesting to note that Caleb's grandmother was named Ephratah (2:50), the ancient name of Bethlehem (Gen. 35:16). Another of Caleb's descendants was actually named Bethlehem (2:51, 54; 4:4). Since David and Nabal both belonged to the tribe of Judah, and since David was born in Bethlehem, perhaps the two men were distant relatives! If so, then David had a double claim on Nabal's hospitality. Note that David referred to himself as Nabal's "son" (v. 8), which suggests that he expected fatherly care from Nabal.

3. "This iniquity" may have included more than Nabal's selfishness and uncharitable attitude. David had taken an oath to slay Nabal and all his men, and it's possible that Abigail somehow heard about it. We get the impression that this wise woman knew what was going on in David's camp. If David didn't keep his oath, foolish as it was, he would sin against the Lord, but Abigail said that she would assume the guilt in his place. Rebekah offered to bear Jacob's curse if her plan failed (Gen. 27:11-13). But if God had wanted David to keep his oath, He would not have intervened as He did.

4. Abishai, Asahel, and Joab were sons of David's sister Zeruiah (1 Chron. 2:16) and nephews of David. Saul's captain Abner killed Asahel, and Joab and Abishai chased him and killed him, much to David's sorrow (2 Sam. 2–3). Abishai became one of David's best military leaders and saved David's life when he was attacked by a giant (2 Sam. 21:15-17).

5. In that day, many people believed that the god you worshiped was limited to the territory of the people who worshiped him, and when you moved to another country, you adopted the gods of that country. Those who worshiped Jehovah had to do it in the land of Israel. David certainly didn't believe this lie but exalted Jehovah as the Lord of all the earth. See Psalms 8, 138–139.

Chapter 11

1. The phrase "keeper of my head" (KJV) means "bodyguard." Had Achish forgotten that David had cut off Goliath's head and kept it? (17:54) Achish's leaders were worried about what David would do with their soldiers' heads (29:4). There's another interesting paradox here. David was Saul's bodyguard (22:14) and Saul didn't trust him, but David was deceiving Achish and the king made him his bodyguard!

2. David left the king as the new day dawned (29:10-11), but Saul was meeting with a witch at night (28:8) and heading for defeat and death.

Chapter 12

1. There is no contradiction between 1 Samuel 28:6 ("When Saul inquired of the Lord") and 1 Chronicles 10:14, that Saul "inquired not of the Lord." Two different Hebrew words are used. In 1 Sam. 28, the word is *sha'al* and means "to ask, to request"; and the word in 1 Chron. 10 is *daresh*, which means "to seek with care." Saul did ask for help but it was not from the heart, nor did he constantly seek God's help as David and Samuel did. He was in trouble, so he called on the Lord.

2. The Hebrews used "sheol" to describe both the grave itself and the realm of the dead. The Greek equivalent is "hades." The bodies of both the saved and the lost go into the grave, but their souls have different destinies. Luke 16:19-31 indicates that sheol/hades was divided into two areas, a place of rest and blessing for the righteous and one of suffering for the wicked. When our Lord ascended to heaven, He emptied the paradise portion and took those souls to heaven. Today, when believers die, they go immediately into the presence of the Lord (2 Cor. 5:1-8). At the judgment of the great white throne, hades will be emptied of the spirits of the lost, and the grave will give up the bodies (Rev. 20:11-18). The unsaved will be found guilty and cast into hell, the lake of fire. Hades is the "jail" but hell is the penitentiary from which none escapes.

3. Saul was one of seven men in Scripture who took their own lives: Abimelech (Jud. 9:54); Samson (Jud. 16:26-30); Saul (1 Sam. 31:4); Saul's armor-bearer (1 Sam. 31:5); Ahithophel (2 Sam. 17:23); Zimri (1 Kings 16:18); and Judas (Matt. 27:6).

Chapter 13

1. *Metropolitan Tabernacle Pulpit*, vol. 48, 521.

2. *The Westminster Pulpit*, vol. 9, p. 17.

3. The name Paul comes from the Latin *paulus*, which means "little, small."

4. George Matheson, *Representative Men of the Old Testament: Ishmael to Daniel* (Hodder and Stoughton, 1900), 173.

Chapter One

The Lord of Hosts Is with Us
(1 Sam. 1-3)

1. Ezekiel became a prophet to his countrymen. Who would you say are our prophets today?

1. How would you describe success?

2. What is the chief factor, according to Wiersbe, of any person's success?

3. What could a modern church leader learn from Samuel to help God's people?

4. What message does God communicate whenever He sends a baby? In 1 Samuel, who was the special baby?

5. How was Hannah a good example of dealing with difficulty?

6. Hannah was criticized as she poured out her heart to the Lord. In what situation have you been criticized when giving your very best to the Lord? How have you handled it?

7. What is most inspiring or instructive to you in Hannah's praise and prayer?

8. What does John Bunyan's quote mean "In prayer it is better to have a heart without words, than words without a heart"?

9. How did Samuel grow up to be godly while his environment was less than ideal? What comfort can this give us for our own children?

10. What four qualities set Samuel apart from Eli?

Chapter Two

Israel's Defeat—God's Victory
(1 Sam. 4–6)

1. Why were the Philistines initially able to defeat God's chosen nation, Israel?

2. When is Satan most likely to be able to gain a foothold in a believer's life?

3. Why didn't it help the Israelites to have the ark of the covenant in the battle with them? How might Christians today make the same type of mistake?

4. How did the Philistines find out that Jehovah God was the true God?

5. How does the incident of the false idol Dagon prostrating before the ark foreshadow the future? (See Phil. 2.)

6. What scheme did the Philistine wise men use to test the Lord?
Why did the Philistines send golden mice and tumors along with the ark?

7. What was the outcome of their scheme?

8. Why didn't the Israelites receive judgment for the improper sacrifices offered after the return of the ark?

9. What lesson do we learn from the fatal mistake of the Israelites who looked into the ark of the covenant?

10. What did the ark of the covenant represent?

Chapter Three

The Call for a King
(1 Sam. 7-11)

1. What did Samuel know was essential for the success of the Israelite nation?

2. What was Israel's besetting sin? What do you believe may be the besetting sin of the modern church?

3. In the broad sense, what is an idol? What or who are you most tempted to serve as an idol?

4. How did the unprepared Israelites defeat the Philistines this time?

5. When you face a battle in your life, what is your strategy?

6. What was Samuel's opinion of the Israelite elders' request for a king? What were the Israelites forgetting?

7. What sometimes happens when the leadership of a church declines spiritually?

8. Although Saul had commendable qualities, what crucial element was Saul missing?

9. After Saul's anointing, what three signs assured him that God truly had chosen him? What three truths about God's care did Saul learn from the signs?

10. How do effective and ineffective leaders differ in how they use their authority? Which type of leader was Saul?

Chapter Four

Reviewing and Rebuking
(1 Sam. 12-13)

1. In order to arrive at the end of our lives not afraid or ashamed, how should we live?

2. What was Samuel trying to teach the Israelites by reviewing their history?

3. How did Israel respond to their national history? Why did they make this mistake again?

4. What should God's people do when they realize they have disobeyed? What hope is there?

5. Part of Samuel's obedience was to pray for the people. How is your practice of prayer?

6. Though methods may change, what spiritual principles should never change for a church or ministry?

7. What were the four downward steps to Saul's failure?

8. How has God tested your faith and patience like God tested Saul? Why does God test His people?

9. What made the difference between Jonathan's victory in battle and Saul's defeat?

10. What has God given us so we can win our spiritual battles? What must we do to receive this?

Chapter Five

A Foolish Vow and a Lame Excuse
(1 Sam. 14-15)

1. What does Wiersbe say are the "three powerful lessons that we must heed and obey if we want the blessing of God on our lives and service"?

2. What enabled Jonathan and his armor bearer to launch such an incredible attack?

3. How is the spiritual condition of our hearts revealed?

4. Why did Saul force such a foolish vow on his army? What were the results?

5. Even though God had commanded complete destruction of the Amalekites, what did Saul spare? What were the consequences of his disobedience?

6. How could you personally apply the truth "to obey is better than sacrifice"?

7. The people thought Saul had won a great victory, but in God's sight Saul was a failure. What was the key difference?

8. How can we make sure not to be a failure in God's sight?

9. What does it mean to be a "living sacrifice"? (Romans 12:1-2)

10. How did Saul's failures fit into God's purposes for Israel?

Chapter Six

God Chooses a King
(1 Sam. 16–17)

1. What do you look for when you search for a leader you can trust?

2. How was David's work as a shepherd used later in his life? How might something small that you are currently doing possibly be used in the future?

3. What was the significance of the anointing of David by Samuel?

4. In what ways was David especially suited for the work God had for him to do?

5. What was the key to David's success, as it was for Joseph, Joshua, Samuel, and others? Is this true for you?

6. What was David's response when he heard Goliath's challenge? What do you think your response would be?

7. What do the ten unbelieving spies (Numbers 13:28-29) have in common with David's family and even King Saul?

8. What is the main point of the account of David and Goliath?

9. Where have you seen God's name ridiculed or blasphemed? What could you have done to set the record straight?

10. What lessons can you be learning in this season of your life to give you stronger faith for times to come?

Chapter Seven

A Jealous King
(1 Sam. 18–19)

1. How did God use Saul's pursuit of David for David's good?

2. In what way can popularity and praise from people test and prepare someone?

3. What is envy? What resulted from Saul's deep envy of David?

4. In what different ways did Saul plot and attempt to kill David?

5. Why weren't any of Saul's plots against David successful?

6. What did Jonathan have to lose by helping David survive?
In view of what was at risk, why did Jonathan do it?

7. How is Satan's influence seen in the life of Saul?

8. How did God protect David and Samuel at Ramah?

9. In what way and when did Saul have miraculous experiences of God's Spirit?

10. What do a person's miraculous experiences tell and not tell about that person's faith and character?

Chapter Eight

David In Exile
(1 S a m . 2 0 - 2 2)

1. Why was it wise and not a lack of faith for David to flee Ramah and hide from Saul?

2. How did Saul express his anger at Jonathan for his friendship with David?

3. In what area was Saul fighting the will of God? What were his chances of success?

4. How was David able to write the psalms of encouragement during his time of exile?

5. What was David's creative solution for his escape from Gath?

6. When have you experienced the truth that the "fear of the Lord conquers every other fear"?

7. What kind of person does God call to be His servant?

8. When there is a scheming leader, what usually follows? Why?

9. How did the high priest Ahimelech defend David and himself?

10. What was the ephod? How did it work? Where do people try to find equivalents of ephods today?

Chapter Nine

David the Deliverer
(1 Sam. 23-24)

1. Reflecting on the Booker T. Washington quote, what obstacles did David face? What obstacles do you face?

2. When have you paused to pray about God's will before an action or a decision? What difference did it make?

3. When are leaders likely to lose their perspective and abuse their authority?

4. Why did David flee from the city of Keilah?

5. How did Jonathan help David find strength in God?

6. How have you or could you help a friend of yours find strength in God? How have others helped you in this way?

7. How did God keep His promise of protection for David when Saul was closing in at "the rock"? What do we learn about God from this?

8. In what way is David's respect for Saul a good example for us and our leaders?

9. What are the three possible levels of the exchange of good and evil between people?

10. Why did David pass up his opportunities to kill Saul? Why is this considered one of David's greatest victories?

Chapter Ten

A Wise Woman and a Foolish King
(1 Sam. 25-26)

1. What does it mean that God is the writer and producer of our life's play?

2. When someone dies (like Samuel), how do people talk and act differently about that person compared to when they were alive?

3. What made Samuel such an excellent mentor and counselor for David?

4. How did the Lord show His mercy to David when David felt angry and vengeful toward Nabal?

5. How did Abigail persuade David not to seek revenge on Nabal? What does this tell you about Abigail?

6. How did David receive Abigail's apology and advice? What does this tell you about David?

7. What two things did David do when he heard of Nabal's death?

8. Why didn't David kill Saul when he got a second chance? Why might God have given David this opportunity?

9. Why did David steal Saul's spear and water jug?

10. How did Saul respond to David's reasoning about Saul's unjust pursuit of him? How much did David believe or trust this response?

Chapter Eleven

Living with the Enemy
(1 Sam. 27:1–28:, 29–30)

1. When God said to David, "Do not be like the horse or like the mule," what did He mean? Which are you most likely to be?

2. Which qualities was David lacking when he decided to flee to Gath?

3. When have you lacked these same qualities and then made a decision that wasn't the best? How did it turn out?

4. What are we doing wrong when we start to slip into despondency?

5. In what ways did David deceive Achish? What was the result?

6. Why did the Amalekites attack Ziklag?

7. What did David do upon discovering his city ruined and the people kidnapped?

8. How did God provide guidance to find the Amalekite camp?

9. What can you trust God to do when you encounter problems and crises?

10. What was David's policy on dividing the spoils of victory? Why did he think this was fair?

Chapter Twelve

The King Is Dead!
(1 Sam. 28:3-25;31; 1 Chron. 10)

1. What brought Saul to the point where God no longer responded to him? Where does God's Word tell us that God will not desert believers?

2. Why was Saul so desperate to speak to Samuel?

3. How do we know that Saul was aware of God's prohibition against consulting mediums and spiritists?

4. Where was Samuel that he could actually speak while deceased? Where do believers and unbelievers go now when they die?

5. Why do you think the medium was shocked when Samuel was called up from the dead and even spoke to Saul?

6. What did the deceased Samuel tell Saul? How did Saul react?

7. What two qualities of faith was Saul missing?

8. In what ways was Saul humiliated even after his death?

9. Why did the men of Jabesh Gilead risk their lives to rescue the bodies of Saul and his sons?

10. What can we learn from the negative example of Saul?

Chapter Thirteen

Four Successes and Two Failures
(Review of 1 Samuel)

1. What is one possible reason God gave Saul to the Israelites as their king?

2. What did Hannah realize that many average people forget? How did Hannah serve God?

3. Despite Eli's failings, what can he be commended for?

4. In what ways is Saul an example to older believers?

5. What was Saul's chief problem? What were his secondary problems?

6. How did Saul's success help bring about his failure? How could it have been different?

7. What examples of good friendship did Jonathan leave behind?

8. Before this study, what did you remember most about David? What have you learned?

9. If someone were to ask you, "What is in 1 Samuel?" how would you answer?

10. What is the key to being truly successful?